Safety Training That Transfers

Steven Cohen and Ellis Ritz

PRESS

ATD Press is an internationally renowned source of insightful and practical
information on workplace learning, training, and professional development.

ATD Press
1640 King Street
Alexandria, VA 22314

Ordering information: Books published by ATD Press can be purchased by visiting
ATD's website at td.org/books or by calling 800.628.2783 or 703.683.8100.

Library of Congress Control Number: 2014949520

ISBN-10: 1-56286-929-9
ISBN-13: 978-1-56286-929-8
e-ISBN: 978-1-60728-504-5

ATD Press Editorial Staff:
Director: Kristine Luecker
Manager: Christian Green
Community of Practice Manager, Learning and Development: Juana Llorens
Associate Editor: Melissa Jones
Text and Cover Design: Marisa Kelly

Printed by Versa Press, Inc., East Peoria, IL, www.versapress.com

Contents

Preface

When we started our business in 2011 we were warned by our first client that the training participants were not going to enjoy activity-focused training. One of the first participants who walked into the room made a sly comment about being back in kindergarten, due to the pipe cleaners, modelling clay, markers, and candy in the room. There were a lot of inquisitive looks and jokes as everyone filtered into our non-traditional training space.

Believing in the power of action-based learning, we kicked off our training session with a bang. Everyone in the room had to stand up, find a partner, stand back to back, and then change five things about their physical appearance. They then turned back around and had to guess what was different. We explained this was not going to be a training program like they had ever experienced and we wanted them to be open to embracing a new style of learning, just as they had been open to engaging in a non-traditional training activity. It only took a few moments for the participants to settle in and connect with the learning at hand.

We were leading a regulatory refresher training course covering mandatory topics relating to certain safety requirements governed by the mining industry. Every year the participants went through the same training, on the same topics, in the same way. That year—in our class—they got a taste of what safety training should be. They learned about awareness through a scavenger hunt, practiced maintaining safe speeds during a relay race, learned about electrical safety by playing the game operation, and even learned about explosive hazards by setting off a blast using Diet Coke and Mentos. There were 75 participants and after the eight-hour session, many of them came up, shook our hands, and thanked us for the best training program they had ever been to.

One of our main reasons for writing this book and sharing our knowledge is to break down the paradigm of how training gets done in many organizations. We have trained hundreds of people during the past few years, and every time, with every client, in every country, we get the same engagement, participation, and feedback—"this was great!" We want to let people know that training does not have to be boring! Boring training is a waste of time, money, energy, and resources. The National Training Laboratories in Bethel, Maine, found that people only retain 5 percent of content when going through a lecture-focused training session. Five percent! After eight hours of being bombarded with information, we only walk away with 5 percent of learned information.

We wrote *Safety Training That Transfers* because conducting sessions that use 300 PowerPoint slides, monotonous lectures, uninspiring deliveries, or outdated and irrelevant information is not training—it is a time waster that needs to be stopped. This is a book for those who think their employees will not embrace and participate in action-based training.

This book is also an acknowledgment that safety training, while often neglected, is an essential part of our work life. Private industry employers reported nearly 3 million nonfatal workplace injuries and illnesses in 2012, according to the Bureau of Labor Statistics. OSHA cites that employers pay almost $1 billion per week for direct workers' compensation costs alone. Safety in the workplace is something we take very seriously and are extremely passionate about. We believe that everyone has the potential to be great; they just need a catalyst to help unlock it. This book is that catalyst. It is a means to help create experiences that can change the way work gets done. It is about creating a workplace where people can do their job in a way that is safe and productive.

Each of the six chapters in this book features activities focused on different aspects of a safety training session. An explanation of the materials, purpose, instructions, and application is provided for each activity.

1. **Materials**

   Most of the materials used in the activities can be found in the majority of work areas, however some items may need to be purchased. This book was not designed to be a spur-of-the-moment resource for on-the-fly training purposes. It will be most useful to those who take the time to read through each activity and understand how it applies to their training needs, identify why it is important, and create a plan for gathering the necessary materials prior to commencing.

2. **Purpose and Overview**

   Malcolm Knowles, the father of adult learning, explains that we have to understand the purpose and benefit before we decide to engage with learning. As adults we need to see some value associated with the things we do. In the purpose and objective sections of each activity, we outline why the activity is important. When conducting your training program, it is important that you spend some time explaining what the participants are about to do and why, before going on to give any directions. Give them the reasons so they understand the value—setting up the activity this way is critical to ensuring your participants fully understand what is being asked of them.

3. **Instructions**

   The directions to our activities have been specifically crafted in a way that allows for clarity and success—we use these setups in our training sessions and they have worked well for us. There is an art to making sure you say the right words when providing directions. Our goal is never to trick our trainees, but to provide them with enough ambiguity that will lead to the outcome we want. It is important, however, that your trainees fully understand what to do. We often have a few participants repeat back exactly what the group will be doing, which is called aligned understanding and will make a significant difference as your trainees go through the exercise.

4. **Delivery**

   There is a difference between doing an activity and playing a game. An activity is a purposeful experience that brings people together for a shared learning experience; a game is something that is done simply for fun. Even though many of our activities are fun, they have an important message or generate an important experience that directly relates to the safety theme. It is critical to debrief the group after every activity, because building the connection between what the participants did and why they learned it is the most important part in executing an effective training activity. Have the group start a dialogue to share their learning experience and help understand its connection to the activity. Application is essential to changing the status quo, but this won't happen unless the learning is internalized and well understood.

As you go through this book we encourage you to remember that the activities, when facilitated correctly, can have a significant impact on your trainees, creating the aha moments required to ensure the application of training in the workplace. These activities are best demonstrated if you fully understand all of their components and introduce them at the right time, to the right audience. They have been designed to not only increase knowledge around important safety topics, but also help build relationships among co-workers and boost morale in the workplace. During our more than 70 years of combined experience operating within dangerous work settings, we have seen what is possible when people are properly trained.

We are confident you will generate the participation, engagement, and dialogue you are looking for and wish you the best of luck. We are excited to be a resource and are open to all inquiries relating to safety or training in the workplace. We look forward to being in touch! Feel free to contact us at steven.cohen@meyvnglobal.com and ellis.ritz@meyvnglobal.com.

—Steve and Ellis

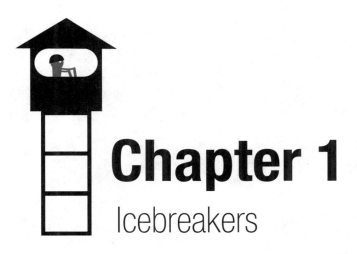

Chapter 1
Icebreakers

An icebreaker is a short activity to establish a healthy learning environment, which should be done immediately following participant introductions. The icebreaker, when possible, should connect with the training theme and start the day with laughter, engagement, and a sense of understanding. Many trainers skip icebreakers and jump right into the content because they think icebreakers are a waste of time. From our experience, however, icebreakers are incredibly important and need to be done at every training program. People are much more likely to stay involved if they are engaged right away. Use these icebreakers to bring the group together early on—they are a great way to kick off your safety training!

Title: Safety Back to Back

Time: 10–15 minutes

Materials:

sticky notes   pens

Purpose:
- Create a friendly environment that is conducive to learning.
- Generate communication and participation early on.
- Solicit participant engagement through Q&A activities.
- Get people thinking critically and expansively about items related to safety.

Overview:

The safety name tag icebreaker immediately initiates engagement among the participants. The setup for this activity is the most important component. The facilitator should think of as many safety items as possible prior to the beginning of the training session. (Some possible safety items are listed in the prep instructions section.)

The key to the success of this activity is how well the facilitator explains its only rule: Each participant can only ask yes or no questions. Ideally, each participant should have to ask at least five or six questions before being able to identify the safety item. As the facilitator, be sure to work the room to enforce the yes or no question rule.

Prep Instructions:

Write the names of safety-related items on sticky notes. There should be more than enough to ensure that everyone in the group gets one.
- Example safety-related items:
  - » flashlight
  - » personal protective equipment (PPE)
  - » fall protection
  - » back-up alarm

- » caution tape
- » signage
- » labels
- » training
- » safety gloves
- » awareness
- » fit for duty

- » sixth sense
- » hearing protection
- » procedure manual
- » eye protection
- » experience
- » teamwork
- » ergonomics.

Activity Directions:

1. Divide the group into pairs and place a sticky note on each participant's back.

2. Explain to each pair that they must work together, asking only yes or no questions, to figure out their safety item.
   - Example questions:
     - » Am I a procedure?
     - » Am I a piece of safety gear?
     - » Am I bright and colorful?

3. Once both partners have identified their safety item, they can sit down. However, if they are unable to identify their safety item after several minutes, they must find new partners and repeat the process until each participant has successfully identified the safety item.

Debrief Questions:

1. What were some of the safety items you guessed and how are they used in the workplace?

2. Why are these safety items so critical to our success?

Title: Once Upon a Time

Time: 10–15 minutes

Materials:

paper   pens   flipchart

Purpose:

- Create a collaborative environment.
- Utilize creative thinking skills while incorporating safety.
- Enable and empower the group to connect through stories.

Overview:

This activity presents a non-threatening way to get participants involved early in the training session. It is easy and does not require a lot of time, yet it helps generate interesting ideas and stories. While the stories are often humorous, they represent important lessons and valuable messages that should be discussed among the participants.

By having each participant take a few moments to create a sentence to add to the story, you are generating creative ideas related to safety. Once each participant has written a sentence, you will share the story with the group and have them discuss the themes presented. By contributing to the story, each participant is able to share his or her knowledge with the group. This is a great way to kick off a safety meeting as the story itself can generate the discussion topics for the session.

Repeating the exercise will lead to new topics for discussion. Encourage the participants to create as many stories as possible within the allotted timeframe. The more stories they generate, the more creative they can become!

Prep Instructions:

Print the sentence "Yesterday, David was working in an unsafe manner and sustained an injury" on a sheet of paper. This sentence will always be the first in this exercise.

. . . .

Activity Directions:

1. Explain to the group that each participant is going to write one sentence that will be added to the content of a story. This story can incorporate anything they want. The only rule is that the story should be related to safety in the workplace.

2. Pass the sheet of paper with the opening sentence on it to someone in the group and have him or her write the second sentence of the story. This sentence can be funny, serious, off-the-wall, or practical. Some examples include:
   - » David was extremely tired after staying up all night watching his favorite football team.
   - » He broke his leg.
   - » He was climbing a ladder when he slipped and fell.

3. Pass the sheet of paper from participant to participant, with each adding a sentence to the story.

4. Once each participant has written a sentence, read the story aloud to the group.

5. Have a participant record (on a flipchart) each safety infraction David committed that led to his injury.

6. Take some time to review the safety infractions identified in the story and conduct a group discussion.

. . . .

Debrief Questions:

1. What are some things David could or should have done to prevent his injury from occurring?

2. How often do these types of injuries occur?

3. Ultimately, why did David get hurt? What led to his injury?

4. Do you face similar scenarios in your work? Where?

Title: Safety Fact or Fiction

Time: 15–20 minutes

Materials:

For each participant you will need:

paper   pens

Purpose:

- Allow participants to share some information about themselves.
- Create a fun and engaging atmosphere.
- Generate numerous safety themes in a short period of time.
- Get people thinking critically about what safety scenarios are realistic.

Overview:

In this icebreaker activity the participants will share three safety-related practices—two they follow and one they don't—with the group and have the group decide which one is not followed.

A good best practice is for the facilitator to provide context by sharing his or her own personal scenarios. This will help the participants understand the specifics of the exercise. The more creative and "out there," the facilitator's scenarios are, the more creative and "out there" the participants' scenarios will be.

This icebreaker activity may be difficult for some participants because it requires them to recall safety-related scenarios that have personally affected or involved them. It is important for the facilitator to provide the group with ample time to come up with relevant scenarios—do not rush the participants. If participants are struggling to recall three scenarios, have them provide two scenarios, one fact and one fiction.

- -

Activity Directions:

1. Explain that the participants should select two safety-related procedures they follow in the workplace (fact) and one safety-related procedure that they do not currently follow (fiction).

   - Examples:
     » I always wear my seatbelt when driving in my vehicle (fact).
     » I wear my hard hat whenever I am working near falling hazards (fact).
     » I check my tire pressure daily (fiction).

2. Ask a participant to share three safety scenarios.

3. Go around the room and have each participant decide which scenario is fiction.

4. Have the original participant reveal which scenario was fiction.

5. Repeat the process until all the participants have shared their stories.

- -

Debrief Questions:

1. What were the most common scenarios?

2. Who presented the most difficult scenario to identify as fiction?

3. What were some of the most important safety procedures revealed during this activity?

4. What scenarios could you use to further discussions about safety procedures?

Title: Safety Names

Time: 5–15 minutes

Purpose:

- Learn each participant's name.
- Create an association between a name and safety tool.
- Build a rapport between the participants.

Overview:

Name association is a great tool to help people remember names. This is a quick ice-breaker that is focused primarily on having the participants learn each other's names, as well as safety items used in the workplace. When participants call one another by their first names, it allows for a more connected and intimate group.

- -

Activity Directions:

1. Arrange the group into a circle around the room.

2. Ask each participant to come up with a safety-related item that begins with the same letter as the first letter of his or her name.

   - For example:
     » Steve: Stop (if you stop before conducting work, you can check for possible hazards).
     » Derrick: Down (if you down equipment when something is not safe, you can prevent injury and incidents).
     » Amy: Awareness (the more aware you are, the safer you, and those working around you, will be).

3. Start by saying your first name and a safety item that begins with the same letter (Steve Stop). Explain your safety item.

4. Have the person sitting to the left of you repeat your first name and safety item, and then follow with his or her name and corresponding safety item.

5. Continue around the circle until the last participant has repeated everyone's name and safety item and then his or her name and safety item.

    - Example:
        » Steve is the facilitator and starts by saying "Steve Stop."
        » Then it is Derrick's turn—he says, "Steve Stop, Derrick Down."
        » Then it is Amy's turn—she says, "Steve Stop, Derrick Down, Amy Awareness."

. . . .

Debrief Questions:

1. How many people can recite everyone's name and safety tool?

2. Which of the safety tools mentioned should we be using on a regular basis?

3. How can you ensure you are consistently using the safety tools mentioned in the workplace?

Title: Guess the Person

Time: 10–20 minutes

Materials:

For each participant you will need:

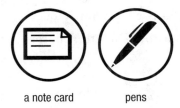

a note card   pens

Purpose:

- Allow participants to get to know one another.
- Share commonalities with other participants.
- Facilitate participation and self-sharing at the beginning of a training session.

Overview:

In this activity the participants document some safety information relevant to their job, experience, and work environment on a note card. The goal is to look for and create habits that deter complacency in the workplace.

A note card could include:

- Have been a Triple Zero safety award winner for the past 10 years.
- Responsible for inspecting all fire extinguishers in my work area for damage every week.
- Once performed CPR on a co-worker who had sustained a significant injury.
- Responsible for inspecting the scaffolding used every day.
- Drive slow during harsh weather conditions.
- Inspect the workplace prior to beginning work in order to identify potential hazards.

Prep Instructions:

Prepare your card prior to introducing the activity. You can use it as an example to elicit more appropriate responses from the participants.

• •

Activity Directions:

1. Pass out a note card and pen to each participant.

2. Share your card with the group.

3. Ask the participants to write three interesting facts about the safety aspects of their jobs and/or any safety facts other participants may not know about them. The more obscure and unique the information, the better it will be for the activity.

4. Give the group a few minutes to write down their safety facts and then ask them to form a circle.

5. Have the participants mingle around the circle continuously exchanging cards with one other. The participants should always have one card in their hand and should not be holding their own card when time is called.

6. After 60 seconds, call time and ask the group to form another circle.

7. Ask for a volunteer to read the card he or she is holding. Then ask the group, "Who do you think wrote this card?"

8. Have the group guess the author of the card, and say why. Then ask the author to come forward. Repeat the process until all the cards have been read.

• •

Debrief Questions:

1. What were some of the safety commonalities we share in our roles?

2. Who was the hardest person to identify?

3. What safety procedures would you like to adopt after learning about each person's safety responsibilities?

Title: Safety Ball Toss

Time: 5–10 minutes

Materials:

| ball (tennis ball, stress ball, bouncy ball, or soccer ball) | stopwatch, timer, or watch with a seconds hand | flipchart | pens |

Purpose:
- Learn everyone's name.
- Think about safety terms under pressure (thinking quickly on your feet).
- Grow together through seeing and experiencing improvement during a timed task.
- Allow group members to create a strategy and foster their ability to work and collaborate in a team setting.

Overview:

This activity creates a competitive environment in which group members must battle against the clock while completing a task. There is a strategic component involved here—thinking through safety items and reciting these items out loud in front of the group.

This activity is focused primarily on process improvement and continuous improvement. The act of conscious, continuous improvement will often lead to improved safety, as people will identify better ways for getting things done. Encouraging participants to have a mindset that is focused on continuous improvement will allow for updated procedures and processes, identification of new tools, and positive change to be made in the workplace.

• •

Activity Directions:

1. Arrange the participants in a circle. Have everyone spaced so they have plenty of room and are not standing shoulder-to-shoulder.

2. Hold the ball while explaining the rules of the activity.
   - Rules:
     » You must hold the ball with both hands.
     » While holding the ball, say your name and a word associated with safety, then pass the ball to the next person.
       ▪ Example: Mark, Training
     » Time starts when I say "Go!" and pass the ball to the first participant.
     » Time stops when the last participant says his or her name and a safety word or item.
     » During the activity, I will record the safety terms mentioned by each of you on the flipchart.

3. Once the first trial has been completed, announce the time taken to complete the activity and then encourage the participants to perform the activity again at a faster pace. Give the participants two to three minutes to think about and discuss how they can improve their process and time.

4. Repeat the process three to four times and document the time improvements. Observe and make note of the adjustments the participants make on their own (saying their names faster, standing closer together in a circle, and so on).

5. A challenge for subsequent rounds—intended to prompt the participants to think more comprehensively about safety—is to explain that each person must say a different safety term or item than one used during the previous round.
   - Example: If Jane says "awareness" in round 1 and "proper lighting" in round 2, she cannot use either of these terms in round 3.

• •

Debrief Questions:

1. What are some of the things you did to improve your time?

2. What are some of the things you can do in the work area to improve safety?

3. What are some of the things you can do to improve productivity and efficiency?

4. How can you increase the level of safety consciousness in the workplace?

5. Why is it so critical to have a mindset focused on continuous improvement?

Title: Impairment

Time: 10–12 minutes

Materials:

drug testing
policy

For each participant you will need:

paper   markers

Purpose:
- Reinforce the importance of being fit for duty.
- The dangers of working while not operating at 100 percent.

Overview:

This activity represents what happens when we are not operating at our maximum ability due to impairment. Most people know the serious safety concerns associated with operating under the influence of alcohol or drugs, but people rarely think about the impact of tiredness and prescription medication side effects.

When we are not operating at 100 percent we put others and ourselves in danger due to impairment. This activity is focused on showcasing the results of what happens when operating impaired.

Activity Directions:

1. Pass out a piece of paper and a marker to everyone in the group.

2. Explain that in this activity group members are going to conduct an easy task—writing a basic sentence on the piece of paper.

3. Ask the participants to write the following sentence with their **non-dominant hand**: When I come to work it is critical I am always fit for duty!
   - This represents impairment. It helps demonstrate how when we are impaired, even basic, easy, everyday tasks can be hard to complete.

4. Have group members show each other the sentences they wrote.
   - The sentences will be out of line, the letters might look strange, and the quality of the work will have suffered.

5. Ask the group questions to continue the dialogue around the importance of being fit for duty at work.

Debrief Questions:

1. What are some things that can prevent us from being fit for duty?

2. What does your fit for duty policy state?

3. What should you do if you are not feeling fit for duty?

4. What should you do if you are concerned someone at work is not fit for duty?

Title: Focused Listening

Time: 10–15 minutes

Materials:

stopwatch
or clock with a
seconds hand

Purpose:
- Learn and hone active listening and communication skills.

Overview:

Listening is so much a part of everyday life that we rarely stop and think about how to do it well. Our ability to listen helps prevent incidents in the workplace by allowing us to gather proper directions, hear abnormal noises, and communicate effectively with our peers. This activity gives participants a chance to really think about what it feels like to listen closely and allows them to practice their listening skills.

• •

Activity Directions:

1. Divide the group into teams of two.

2. Ask each team to select a topic for discussion. The topic can be anything (a favorite holiday, favorite vacation, family, or similar).

3. Explain that one person in each pair will talk to his or her partner for five minutes about a topic of choice. The listening partner cannot interrupt for any reason. No questions. No clarifying. No talking of any kind.

4. Have the pairs switch roles and repeat step 3.

5. Once both parties have spoken, facilitate a group discussion about the role of just listening.

· ·

Debrief Questions:

1. Were you able to remain focused the whole time?

2. Did you want to ask any questions?

3. How can you improve your listening skills?

4. How can you improve your communication skills?

Chapter 2
General Safety

The activities in this section are each tied to a specific safety theme and will work great in toolbox or safety meeting settings. Some of the topics relate to identifying safety tools in the workplace, emergency evacuation, awareness, barricading, and labeling. These general topics are relevant for most work environments and should be used to share safety information. If your organization has specific policies and procedures associated with these safety topics we encourage you to incorporate those into the activity.

Title: Pick a Pic

Time: 10–15 minutes

Materials:

| printed out pictures of different safety items | masking tape | markers |

Purpose:
- Communicate the importance of using various safety tools.
- Create awareness around safety in the workplace.
- Start conversations about the tools that are the most essential to safety.

Overview:

This activity requires very little setup and can help generate great safety discussions. By understanding what tools are available, where they are located, and how to use each one properly, the participants will gain a better awareness of their workplace.

This activity allows each person to share something related to safety. In addition, since the participants identify their favorite safety tool from the ones displayed on the wall, it helps identify which safety tools the participants believe are the most important. If one picture receives the majority of votes, it is essential to discuss why that is.

Prep Instructions:

Arrange pictures of safety items in an area where the participants can both see and access them.

- You could print out the pictures and tape them to the wall or make a collage with many pictures in a word document and then use a projector to display that on a screen or blank wall.
- Example images include:

» hard hat

» two-way radio

» fall protection

» SOP (standard operating procedure)

» headlamp

» wheel chocks.

. . . .

Activity Directions:

1. Have the participants mark their favorite (or the most practical) safety item used in the workplace with a piece of masking tape bearing their name.

2. Ask each participant to explain why he or she chose the safety item and how it is beneficial in the workplace.

3. If appropriate, facilitate a discussion to identify and explain the different uses and advantages of each safety item. After at least 10 minutes of discussion, use the debrief questions to further develop your conversion.

. . . .

Debrief Questions:

1. When should each item be used or not be used?

2. How does each item keep us safe?

3. Where should these items be located on the job site or in the workplace?

4. Which items require training prior to use?

Title: The Three Questions Game

Time: 5–10 minutes

Materials:

For each team you will need:

paper   markers

Purpose:

- Promote teamwork and collaboration by working together in small groups.
- Allow for safety commonalities to be identified and discussed.
- Use repetition as a retention tool and challenge the group to think outside the box.

Overview:

Repetition is a great retention tool. This activity requires a great deal of collaboration and repetition regarding safety topics. Every topic has different facets and this activity brings many unique perspectives together in a short period of time. When they're encouraged to make the connections around safety topics, the participants will begin to see safety from different angles.

• •

Activity Directions:

1. Split the group into teams of four participants or less.

2. Have each team think of three different safety questions that have the same answer. Ask the team members to collaborate to come up with the most creative questions possible.
    - Example questions:
      » Where can hazardous materials be stored underground?
        ▪ Answer: storage facility.

» What area is routinely forgotten about but may store essential materials?

- Answer: storage facility.

» If you were going to keep flammable items in the same place, what would you need?

- Answer: storage facility.

3. Ask each team to read its questions to the rest of the group and explain the safety-related procedures and topics that go along with each.

. . . .

Debrief Questions:

1. What were your three questions?

2. What is the safety relevance of the items answered in your questions?

3. When should we be using these items?

4. How often are you asking safety questions?

5. What safety questions should you be asking on a regular basis?

Title: Safety Scavenger Hunt

Time: 15–20 minutes

Materials:

For each team you will need:

| paper | markers | printed list of questions | digital camera, smartphone, or tablet |

Purpose:

- Locate important safety items within the workplace.

Overview:

A scavenger hunt can be set up quickly and without much effort. This activity allows participants to become very familiar with their work area to minimize complacency. The facilitator can modify the activity to cater to a specific work area, or use the questions suggested in the following prep instructions section for a more generic session.

The facilitator should think through the important safety items that are specific to and necessary within the featured work area. The more questions and areas provided, the more productive the activity will be. It is important to note that this activity should not be conducted at a table, but rather, physically out and about. The group should be walking to all of the exits, going to see where the first aid kit is located, walking to the emergency evacuation sheets, and so forth. Having the participants move will allow for an energy release and some physical activity. Photo documentation will provide proof that the team physically visited each area.

Prep Instructions:

Print out the following list of questions or come up with different questions tailored to a specific work environment:

- Where is the closest fire extinguisher?
- Where are the evacuation plans located?
- Where are the exits in the building?
- Where is the muster point (designated gathering spot away from the building) for this building?
- Where are emergency contact numbers located? What are they?
- What signage is present in the work area?
- Where is the first aid kit located?
- Where is the designated smoking area?

• •

Activity Directions:

1. Divide the participants into teams and provide each team with a list of questions, a marker, and a camera. Tell them to get creative!

2. Explain to the teams that they will be participating in a scavenger hunt within the building in which they work. The teams will walk to the various areas described in the questions, recording their answers and documenting their findings with a photograph.

   - Encourage team creativity while taking photos—include the members of the group demonstrating the proper use of a safety item or the proper assembly within a safety location.

3. The first team to locate and document all items on the list is the winner.

4. Have the teams share their answers and photos once all the teams have returned.

   - There can be a creativity element added to this activity—have the group vote on the most creative photo, best illustration of proper use of the safety item, best reenactment of the reason for using a safety item or location, and so on.

• •

Debrief Questions:

1. What questions did you have a hard time answering?

2. What are some of the other items in the workplace that you should know the location of?

3. How do we ensure that all the items in the scavenger hunt are in compliance and inspected regularly?

4. Were we missing any of the items included in the scavenger hunt, and if so, what do we need to do?

Title: Highs and Lows

Time: 20–25 minutes

Materials:

flipchart   markers

Purpose:

- Acknowledge the benefits and challenges posed by safety processes.
- Identify some of the obstacles that can be generated by working safely and following safety protocols.
- Discuss solutions for some of the difficulties associated with safety procedures and equipment.

Overview:

Safety must be the bedrock of everything done on the worksite. But, while entirely necessary, safety is not without its frustrations. Doing things safely might mean that tasks take longer to complete, workers have to wear uncomfortable equipment like harnesses and PPE (personal protective equipment), and, most importantly, the "traditional" way of doing things may have to be altered. Change is uncomfortable and not intuitive for most people.

This activity examines the not-so-favorable aspects of working safely, and forces participants to think about ways to overcome safety obstacles. The facilitator will write down the solutions generated by the group on the flipchart. A good follow-up action is to use these solutions to create specific action items addressing each of the issues identified.

Activity Directions:

1. Explain that each participant is responsible for thinking of at least one high and one low point related to working safely.

- Example high points:
  - » Prevents injuries.
  - » Allows me to go home to my family each day.
  - » Radio communication ensures effective teamwork.
  - » Following standard operating procedures limits rework.
- Example low points:
  - » PPE can be uncomfortable.
  - » Wearing a hard hat all day can get hot.
  - » Certain tasks might take longer to do.
  - » Conducting inspections can be time consuming.

2. Have the participants share their high and low points regarding safety requirements related to their specific job.

3. As each participant shares his or her low point, facilitate a discussion about how this aspect of the job could be improved. For example, you could remedy an uncomfortable hard hat by reviewing the different brands available and how to properly fit a hard hat to make it more comfortable.

· ·

Debrief Questions:

1. What did you identify as your highs?

2. How can you overcome the lows identified?

3. How do you stay connected to the highs to ensure you are constantly operating with a safety-conscious mind?

Title: Reaction

Time: 10–25 minutes

Materials:

For each participant you will need:

a picture of
a common
scenario in the
workplace

Purpose:

- Identify people's initial responses to a critical situation.
- Identify correct and incorrect reactions.
- Tailor the training to fill the gaps between incorrect and correct reactions.

Overview:

This activity allows the facilitator to immediately identify opportunities for training. By preventing participants from thinking through a scenario the facilitator provides a realistic representation of what each participant would do in a real-life situation. This is critically important to identify, because how the situations presented in this activity are handled can be the difference between life and death.

A key to this activity's success is finding pictures or images that represent practical scenarios that could realistically occur in the workplace. These scenarios can be general —such as a workplace injury, property damage, slipping hazard due to a wet area, or an open hole—or they can be more specific to the workplace role of the participants.

The facilitator must also make sure that participants understand that they will have no time to think through what to do; they should react immediately (impulsively) to the scenario.

NOTE: Don't include pictures of safety procedures that participants haven't been trained on. The reaction activity is best used as a review to check for understanding after the procedures have been taught.

Prep Instructions:

1. Gather images or documents with words depicting scenarios common in the workplace. Have one for each participant.
   - Potential scenarios might include:
     - » someone working at heights without fall protection
     - » fire
     - » chemical leak
     - » working under a suspended load
     - » light duty vehicle accident.

2. Place the images and documents face down on a table prior to introducing the activity.

- -

Activity Directions:

1. Have a participant choose a piece of paper and turn it over to reveal the safety hazard.

2. Ask the participant to react according to how he or she would respond if the occurrence was happening in the workplace.
   - Example: combustible materials:
     - » Participant could pretend to call a supervisor or use a fire extinguisher to put out a fire.

3. Upon completion of the scenario, take some time as a group to critique the participant's actions, address any changes that should be made to the reaction, and then thank the participant for his or her efforts.

4. Continue the activity until each participant has had a chance to choose an incident and react accordingly.

- -

Debrief Questions:

1. What were your reactions?

2. Were there images you had a hard time coming up with a solution for?

3. What allows us to react positively or negatively when facing a situation in the field?

4. Is it better to react right away or step back and think about our upcoming actions?

Title: Safety Four Square

Time: 15–25 minutes

Materials:

For each participant you will need:

sketch paper
(oversized sheet
of paper)

markers

Purpose:

- Clarify important safety concepts at work.
- Create a diverse product encompassing all aspects of safety.
- Allow for independent work and introspection regarding safety and what it means.

Overview:

Safety is composed of more than simply following necessary procedures. It is a mindset, a value, and something that is internal and all encompassing. This activity breaks down the main components of safety in a way that allows for participant introspection.

Safety is important on many levels. Creating a visual representation of the four main components of safety can inspire the participants and provide them with a deeper sense of understanding. The four components of the safety four square are founded on the following questions:

1. Why do I decide to work safely?
    - purpose:
        » family
        » friends
        » pets
        » desire to live
        » protect my co-workers.

2. What do I do every day to ensure I work safely?

- attitude:
  - » get a good night's sleep
  - » make sure I am fit for duty
  - » conduct all of my necessary inspections before starting work
  - » make sure I have been properly trained for my task
  - » gain clarity on my responsibilities for the day.

3. What tools are available to me to ensure I work safely?

- resources:
  - » PPE
  - » standard operating procedures
  - » reflective clothing
  - » radio
  - » signage.

4. What do I need in my work environment to ensure I work safely every day?

- culture:
  - » good leadership
  - » the ability to speak up when I see something unsafe, without retaliation
  - » positive recognition
  - » updates from my supervisor
  - » team mentality of safeguarding; a sense of responsibility for each other.

Prep Instructions:

Create your own safety four square before this activity to use as an example.

• •

Activity Directions:

1. Pass out sketch paper and markers to each participant and instruct the group to fold their piece of paper into quarters, creating four squares.

2. Ask the participants to write one question in each of the four squares (see below). Tell them to leave plenty of space under the question, because they

will be drawing or writing their answers to these questions.

- Top left quadrant: Why do I decide to work safely?
- Top right quadrant: What do I do every day to ensure I work safely?
- Bottom left quadrant: What tools are available to me to ensure I work safely?
- Bottom right quadrant: What do I need in my work environment to ensure I work safely every day?

3.   Give the group 10 minutes to draw or record their four corner safety items. When time is up, have the participants share their answers.

• •

Debrief Questions:

1.   Use the items the participants drew or recorded to introduce themes and review content introduced during the activity.

2.   Which question was the hardest to answer and why?

3.   Were there certain tools you identified that you currently do not possess?

4.   Were there certain items you require in your work that you currently do not possess?

5.   What are some things you currently do not do every day, but should, to ensure you work safe all the time?

Title: Finish the Safety Phrase

Time: 10–15 minutes

Purpose:
- Ensure that the appropriate knowledge level exists regarding specific safety procedures.
- Use a quiz-style approach to test knowledge.

Overview:

This activity must be customized to the specific procedures, standards, and best practices associated with the participant's work responsibilities. This is a less formalized way to ensure that participants fully understand the processes specific to their work responsibilities.

The key to the success of this activity is customizing it to each specific participant audience. The facilitator must be familiar with the standard operating procedures (SOP) for each participant and should pull the questions from those procedures. The longer the list of questions, the better prepared the facilitator will be. This list can be used over the course of several weeks.

To modify this activity slightly, the facilitator can pair up the participants and have them identify the answers together.

Prep Instructions:

Generate a list of questions specific to the SOPs of the participants.
- Before turning the key in the ignition, I should always . . .
- When pulling in or backing out of a shop, I should always . . .

• •

Activity Directions:

1. Decide whether to pair participants or have them work independently.

2. Explain that the objective of the activity is to finish the phrase started by the facilitator.

- Remember, the questions must be specific to the participants.

3. The number of questions asked can vary, based on the amount of time spent discussing the safety answers.

   - If participants respond incorrectly, take extra time to discuss why the response is incorrect, and talk through the proper solution, process, or best practice.

• •

Debrief Questions:

1. What are some common procedures we did not review, but should because they are used on a regular basis?

2. Out of the procedures we reviewed, which steps are most commonly missed?

3. Do we need to take another look at some of the procedures? If so, which ones and why?

Title: Fire Extinguisher Inspection

Time: 10–15 minutes

Materials:

fire extinguisher

Purpose:
- Ensure all extinguishers in the workplace have been properly inspected and are up-to-date.
- Identify what to look for when inspecting a fire extinguisher.
- Explain the regulations associated with fire extinguisher inspection.

Overview:

Not only should you ensure that all extinguishers are inspected properly and in good working order in the event they are needed to fight a fire, but it is also vitally important to ensure that your work area is in compliance with various fire extinguisher regulations. The presence of out-of-compliance extinguishers could be the difference between life and death.

There are many things to look for when inspecting an extinguisher. The key to this activity's success is providing ample time for the participants to fully understand the inspection elements. This will improve their ability to perform comprehensive inspections of all extinguishers in the work area.

• •

Activity Directions:

1. Explain the importance of ensuring that all fire extinguishers are in good working order.
   - Make sure to cover:
     » regulatory compliance

» high site standards

» if damaged, it must be removed or replaced

» if it is not in working order it will be useless in the event of a fire.

2. Ask one of the participants to demonstrate how to properly inspect an extinguisher.

    - Make sure the participant is looking at:

        » hose: cracks or plugging

        » pin: tamper seal

        » tank: dents

        » inspection cards: annual or monthly

        » bottom: corrosion

        » collar around top: tightness

        » extinguisher type:

            ▪ make sure it is right for your type of application

            ▪ check gauge (if applicable).

3. After ensuring the participant has examined all vital components of the extinguisher, have another participant come up and perform the same inspection to ensure repetition and retention.

    - A variation of this step could be to have the second participant inspect a different extinguisher—one that has some safety issues. This offers another way of reinforcing the importance of a careful and focused inspection of each individual extinguisher.

4. Have the participants go out into the work area to locate all the fire extinguishers. Have them conduct a thorough inspection of each extinguisher.

5. Discuss follow-up procedures if any extinguishers are found to be non-compliant.

· ·

Debrief Questions:

1. Who is responsible for inspecting the fire extinguishers?

2. How often should fire extinguishers be inspected?

3. What are the consequences if the fire extinguishers are not properly inspected?

4. Where are fire extinguishers most commonly found in the workplace?

Title: Emergency Evacuation Awareness

Time: 10–15 minutes

Materials:

whiteboard   markers

Purpose:

- Learn where the exits at work are located.
- Practice walking through escape routes.
- Identify the location of all fire extinguishers in the work area.
- Learn the muster point for the work area.

Overview:

It is easy to tell people where the exits are, where the fire extinguishers hang, and where the muster point is located. However, *doing* is what actually enhances the retention of information. Having participants walk their escape route, locate the fire extinguishers, and navigate through the exits to the designated muster point will reinforce correct participant reaction in the event of an emergency, versus fear and confusion.

Parents often practice emergency fire evacuations with their children. They practice staying low, crawling to the various exits, touching the handles to see if the doors are hot, setting up an emergency ladder from the window, and so on. Thankfully, most people never experience a house fire, but if they do, they should feel confident that they know exactly what to do because of the repeated practice.

It is natural to become unnerved upon hearing a non-drill alarm. This is why conducting this safety activity is so important. Fire and evacuation drills may seem basic, trivial, or unimportant, but understanding what to do when an evacuation is actually necessary is critical to you and your co-workers' survival.

Prep Instuctions:

Draw out the layout of the work area on the whiteboard. The more details, the better.

. . . .

Activity Directions:

1. Ask the group to tell you where the fire extinguishers are located in the work area.

2. Identify the location of each fire extinguisher in the work area with an "X" on the diagram.

3. Ask the participants to identify all the exits in the work area. Use an "O" on the diagram to identify these.

4. Ask the group where the muster point for their work area is located. Identify this with an "M" on the diagram.

5. Walk the group through a number of scenarios and have the group physically act out the evacuation as if it was a real event.

    - Scenario 1: The alarm goes off, but there is no sign of fire and all exits are clear.

    - Scenario 2: There is smoke coming from the northeast section of the work area and one of the exits is blocked.

    - Scenario 3: Only one exit is clear and the fire has spread through the majority of the building.

    - Scenario 4: A fire breaks out, but the extinguisher is inaccessible, only one exit is free, and many people are trapped.

    - Scenario 5: Create your own realistic scenario requiring an emergency evacuation that might occur in the workplace.

6. For more practice, you can ask the participants to think of additional scenarios.

    - This can elevate engagement and retention, as well as address concerns held by the participants.

. . . .

Debrief Questions:

1. On a scale of 1–10 (with 1 being low and 10 being high) how confident are you that we would effectively evacuate this work area in the event of an emergency? What is your reasoning?

2. How often should we be practicing our emergency evacuation procedure?

3. In the event of an evacuation, what are some of the things that can go wrong, preventing you from following the procedure?

4. How can you stay calm and collected when facing an evacuation?

Title: Tool Identification: The Right and Wrong Way to Use a Tool

Time: 5–15 minutes

Materials:

You will need one commonly misused tool per participant, such as:

small sling   crescent wrench   pliers

Purpose:

- Communicate the importance of using the correct tool for the job.
- Raise awareness surrounding the ramifications of using the right or wrong tool for the task at hand.
- Identify the value of conscious acknowledgment to use the correct tool for each task.

Overview:

In the workplace today, many of us are asked to accomplish more with less (resources, time, space, and so on). There can be grave consequences if you do something as seemingly innocent as taking a shortcut or using the wrong tool in order to complete a task more quickly or easily. The downstream effects can have lasting repercussions for personnel and the company. The extra seconds taken to locate the correct tool can save time, money, and even life and limb.

Activity Directions:

1. Divide the participants into groups of four to five people.

2. Distribute the tools to each group. (Provide one tool to each participant on each team.)

3. Have the participants discuss scenarios where each of their tools have been used incorrectly to complete a task. Participants should also discuss the correct usage of each tool.

45

4. Ask the participants to think about incidents, accidents, or errors that have occurred as the result of using the wrong tool to complete a task.

    • The tools most often misused include using crescent wrenches as hammers, the wrong sling, or pliers to remove nuts and bolts.

5. Come back together and have the participants share what they discussed with their groups.

    • Take 10 minutes for this discussion.

• •

Debrief Questions:

1. What contributes to a decision to use the wrong tool?

2. Is it a conscious decision? (Discussions can be had around both yes and no responses.)

3. What are the potential ramifications of such shortcuts?

4. What are the benefits of selecting the correct tool?

Title: Safe Access Demonstration

Time: 10–12 minutes

Materials:

Items to construct a pathway, hinder safe access, and represent unsafe access points, including:

chairs	backpacks	boxes	ladders	pylons
construction cones	packing popcorn to represent snow or mud			

Purpose:

- Identify what constitutes a safe access way.
- Understand the standard for a safe access way.
- Impart the value of maintaining safe access ways.

Overview:

This activity requires little setup and can serve as a conduit for an expanded discussion regarding the many different points of access at work that require maintenance and awareness of safe accessibility.

There is a need for safe access to the workplace, as well as a need for safe and immediate access to the tools and means for keeping employees safe on the job. Both are paramount to overall workplace safety.

• •

Activity Directions:

1. Have participants place the objects in workplace areas that could create or constitute a violation of safe access, including:
    - in front of a doorway
    - in front of a fire extinguisher
    - in front of first aid materials
    - along a path that would restrict someone from being able to access a doorway
    - spills or mud/snow on a walkway.

2. Ask the participants to identify the reasons why each object (or lack thereof) creates a barrier, and describe what safe access means to them.

• •

Debrief Questions:

1. Is permanent or temporary access provided for all working places?

2. Are employees required to climb equipment or machinery to access workplaces?

3. Are falling hazards created by a lack of safe access conduits, such as stairways, ladders, ramps, or handholds?

Title: Barricading Demonstration

Time: 10–20 minutes

Materials:

barricading tape   information tag   chairs   markers

Purpose:
- Learn how to set up proper barricades in the workplace.
- Understand the importance of utilizing barricades.

Overview:

When spills happen areas need to be quartered off until the appropriate measures to clean the spill can be made. Barricades are often the go-to choice for making a potentially dangerous situation safer. However, they only serve their full purpose if the appropriate signage is used. Too often people barricade an area and consider the job done once the caution tape is up—this activity reminds people that there is more to barricading than caution tape.

Prep Instructions:

1. Take two chairs and place them five steps apart.
2. Connect the barricade tape to each chair, creating a barricade.
   - NOTE: You can also choose to recreate the type of barricade used at the participants' site.

• •

Activity Directions:

1. Ask the participants to create the appropriate signage to display on the barricade. It should include:

- contact number of person in charge
- list of names of people working in the area
- reason the area is barricaded
- date and time the barricade was put up
- reflective properties (if up at night).

2. Inspect the barricade to ensure it is secure and is clearly visible from all directions.

3. Explain the difference between yellow and red caution tape.

4. Discuss what happens if the barricade is going to be in place long term. In this case, the next shift must replace all contact and personnel information. If the barricade is left in place overnight, it must be illuminated, and the use of blinking lights or strobes is advised.

· ·

Debrief Questions:

1. When should we barricade?

2. Did you incorporate everything you were supposed to in the barricade?

3. Who is allowed to create a barricade?

4. How do we prevent people from coming into the barricaded zone when they are not supposed to?

Title: Water, Water Everywhere

Time: 10–15 minutes

Materials:

| five disposable cups | different water sources | drinking fountain | tap water | toilet water | non-potable water |

Purpose:

- Realize the importance of following safety standards pertaining to drinking water in the workplace.
- Create awareness around drinking water, which is something we don't typically think about in regard to safety.
- Engage the group's assumptions regarding the availability of clean, potable water.
- Create awareness surrounding non-potable water (especially that the clarity of the water is not always an indicator that it is potable).
- Identify what constitutes non-potable water.

Overview:

Water quality safety is something that most people in the United States take for granted. For most of the world's population, however, access to clean potable water is not guaranteed. Similarly, under certain circumstances and situations at mining or industrial worksites, the quality of accessible potable water on the work site may be compromised. Awareness is essential—never simply assume.

Water isn't always safe, and things that seem benign can potentially pose a danger. In this activity participants consider the importance of the origin of the water they are working with.

Prep Instructions:

Fill five cups with water from different locations.

- They do not all need to be from sanitary sources, because the participants will not be drinking the water.

- -

Activity Directions:

1. Ask the participants if they know the origin of the water in each cup, and whether they would be willing to drink water with an unknown origin.

2. Reveal where the water in each cup came from.

3. Stress the importance of the drinking water and hygiene standard at the participants' workplace. Emphasize that the standard must be followed in order to deliver safe drinking water to employees on the work site.

- -

Debrief Questions:

1. How often do you question the source of your water supply?

2. Do you know where to find potable water at your work site?

3. Do you know the sources of non-potable water at your work site?

4. How will you change your approach to proper water safety?

Title: Let's Label

Time: 12–17 minutes

Materials:
For each team you will need:

masking tape   colored markers
(a different color
for each team)

Purpose:
- Learn best practices for labeling areas and items to ensure a safe working environment.

Objective:

Labeling is not the most glamorous safety precaution to take. It can be time consuming and can seem redundant or childish. However, clear labels are an important part of a safe working environment. This activity gets people used to labeling, and requires them to talk about what labels are necessary.

• •

Activity Directions:

1. Divide the group into teams of four to five people.

2. Give each team some tape and a different colored marker.

3. Explain that the teams are going to engage in a competition to see which team can apply the most labels to items located in the work area.
   - The more items that are labeled, the better.
   - This activity will allow each participant to create labels and become aware of what can, and should, be labeled.

4. Give the teams five to 10 minutes to apply labels to as many items as possible within the workplace.

5. When time is called, go through the workplace, tally up the number of labels created by each team, and announce the winner.

6. Remove the unnecessary labels and keep the labels that make sense in place.
    • The work area should now have more items labeled than before the activity.

• •

Debrief Questions:

1. What needs labeling in the work area?

2. Who will be responsible for conducting a labeling audit to see what needs to be labeled?

3. Why is proper labeling so important?

4. Does anyone have stories of people getting hurt or sick due to missing labels?

Chapter 3
Team Building

All these activities have an underlying theme of collaboration. In most hazardous work environments people work in teams. These activities are great for employees who are dependent on their peers to complete tasks. These longer activities build relationships and ensure team health by teaching effective communication, trust building, and problem solving.

Title: Safety Memories

Time: 10–15 minutes

Materials:

whiteboard   markers
or flipchart

Purpose:

- Think of safety away from work.
- Share some history about each participant.
- Make the connection that even as children, many of us were utilizing safety procedures to prevent injury.
- Think about how ingrained and natural some safety thinking is in our lives.

Overview:

The main goal of this activity is to have participants introduce themselves to the group, but with the unique twist of talking about safety as a kid. There were plenty of things we did to prevent injuries as we were growing up, and many of them were very funny.

For example, I remember jumping out of our two-story bedroom windows as a child. We took some (highly suspect) safety precautions—we stacked multiple mattresses below the window to support our fall. Sharing childhood memories will help to break the ice and allow for rapport to be built among participants.

It is also useful to talk about how we have matured since those "wild" days and how safety has become more prominent in our day-to-day lives.

Prep Instructions:

Write the following questions on a whiteboard or flipchart:

- What is your name?
- Where do you work (which department)?

- Where did you grow up?

- What is your favorite memory of where you grew up?

- Describe a safety practice you followed as a child to prevent injuries from happening.

• •

Activity Directions:

1. As the facilitator, it is your responsibility to start the icebreaker by answering the questions first.

    - A good example might be if someone grew up in the South, where the heat can pose life-threatening issues—he could explain that proper air-conditioning is an essential safety item.

2. Ask for a volunteer to go next. Have that person answer the questions.

3. Continue the process until each participant has shared his or her answers to the questions.

4. Record the safety items mentioned so that you can use them later to tie them into the meeting's training topic.

    - The air-conditioning example listed above could be related to the importance of underground ventilation systems for miners or staying cool when working in the heat.

• •

Debrief Questions:

1. What were some of the common themes identified in this activity?

2. What did you learn about the people in this room?

3. Which of these themes come into play in your current work environment and how do you prevent these themes from causing harm?

Title: Wordless Safety

Time: 10–15 minutes

Purpose:
- Have the participants bond over an activity that fosters collaboration.
- Instill group ownership by having the group create their own safety-related procedure.
- Allow the participants a creative means of communication through the use of charades or drawing pictures.

Overview:

Due to the nature of this activity, participants may take the easy, fun route, or the more difficult route depending on how well they know one another. This activity requires participants to communicate without using spoken words. Instead, they must use gestures, drawings, acting, and so forth to convey their message.

This activity can be done using drawings or not, it is up to the facilitator to decide. Not allowing drawings will foster more interesting interaction. However, if the participants do not know each other well, you may want to allow drawings to make the group more comfortable. To make the activity easier, you can also provide each group member with a procedure to illustrate.

Prep Instructions:

If you are providing the procedures for the participants, write a procedure on a slip of paper. Make sure you have enough for everyone.
- Possible procedures include:
  - » checking tire pressure
  - » emergency evacuation
  - » conducting work area inspection
  - » putting on proper PPE
  - » using three points of contact
  - » using appropriate back-up horn signal (three honks)
  - » inspecting fall protection.

Activity Directions:

1. Tell the participants to think of a certain safety procedure that is utilized in the workplace. (Or provide each group member with a slip of paper with a procedure written on it.)

2. Ask the participants to select a partner.

3. Explain that each participant must convey his or her safety procedure without speaking, by either acting it out or finding some other creative way to communicate it.

4. Have each team act out their procedures in front of the group. The team that guesses both procedures in the least amount of time is the winner.

Debrief Questions:

1. Do you ever have to communicate without using words? When and why?

2. How did you do with this activity? How could you have improved your communication?

3. In general, how is the communication in the workplace?

4. Why is effective communication so critical to success?

Title: Peer Interview

Time: 10–15 minutes

Materials:

For each participant you will need:

paper   pens

Purpose:

- Allow participants to get to know one another in an intimate setting through a formal interview.
- Encourage participants to share their thoughts about safety.
- Collect data focused on key safety discussions.
- Generate fascinating conversations.

Overview:

This activity encourages sharing through a formal interview. The interview questions are pre-generated and will create a brief synopsis of safety in the workplace. It is important for the facilitator to encourage participants to answer all the questions.

It is also important that the interviewers understand that they should document the interviewees' answers. It is not necessary to capture every spoken word, but their notes need to be detailed enough that they can provide a high-level overview of their partners' responses.

Prep Instructions:

Write the following questions on a whiteboard or have them ready in a handout.

1. What are two safety procedures that you consistently perform every day?

2. In your opinion, what are the most important tools you use in your job?

3. Why do you decide to work safely?

4. What can be done to ensure that those who work around you also choose to work safely?

5. What does it mean to you to be your brother's or sister's keeper?

6. What can we do to ensure that everyone we work with is a safety champion?

• •

Activity Directions:

1. Divide the group into pairs and pass out a pen and piece of paper to each participant.

2. Have each team interview one another using the questions you've either written on the whiteboard or given as a handout.

3. Give the participants about five to 10 minutes to interview each other.

4. Go around the room and ask each participant to introduce his or her partner and share the answers to the interview questions.

• •

Debrief Questions:

1. What did you learn about the person you interviewed?

2. What were some of the most important tools identified from the group and do we do a good job of using those tools? Why or why not?

3. As a group, what is the consensus for why we work safe?

4. What do we have to do as a group to ensure we are always looking out for our brothers or sisters?

Title: Pass the Yarn

Time: 15–20 minutes

Materials:

large ball of
yarn or string

Purpose:

- Create a powerful visual associated with being connected through safety.
- Exchange ideas and learn from one another.

Overview:

This is a simple exercise to set up; however if it is not brought home in the right manner, it will seem lackluster. The most important component of this exercise is the closing, because the visual associated with the activity can be significant. Throughout the exercise people pass around a ball of yarn, with each person holding part of the design. At the end of the exercise every person in the group will be physically connected to everyone else through the yarn. As the facilitator it is your job to accentuate the importance of everyone staying connected through safety.

The yarn represents the connection everyone in the group has through safety—when safety is at the forefront, people will remain connected for life. Working in a dangerous setting with others can create a strong bond that can last a lifetime. It takes everyone in the group to commit to safety in order to stay connected; if one person lets go, the whole design falls apart, because the breakdown makes it impossible for the rest of the group to stay connected. Really emphasize this when summarizing the activity.

Activity Directions:

1. Have the participants arrange themselves in a rectangle.

2. You will start with the ball of yarn—introduce your name, say one thing about your position, and share how you contribute to safety.
    - Examples:
        » My name is Jill.
        » I am your facilitator.
        » I contribute to safety by: looking out for those around me.
        » I contribute to safety by: always coming to work fit for duty.
        » I contribute to safety by: asking for help when I need it.
        » I contribute to safety by: asking questions if I am unsure of something.

3. Pass the ball of yarn to any person in the rectangle who is not directly next to you. Make sure that you keep holding onto the yarn, too. This creates a line connecting you to the person you just gave the yarn to.

4. Have the person you passed the yarn to answer the same questions and then pass the yarn to the next participant. This will create a connection between you, the participant who just presented, and a third person who now has the yarn.

5. Continue the process until all the participants in the rectangle have introduced themselves and talked about their safety contributions.

6. Once everyone is finished and is holding a piece of yarn, summarize the significance of this activity: Through safety we are all connected.

7. Then, have someone let go of the yarn.
    - Explain that when even one person is not committed to safety, it is impossible for the workplace as a whole to be connected, because of the breakdown in connection within the group.

Debrief Questions:

1. Why is it so important that we are **all** committed to safety?

2. What happens when some people are committed to safety and others are not?

3. What can we do to make sure we are all always connected to safety like we are now?

Title: Assessing a Situation Before Acting: The Human Knot

Time: 20–30 minutes

Materials:

This activity requires an even number of participants, with a minimum of six and a maximum of 12.

Purpose:

- Teach the benefits of talking through a situation before acting.
- Collaborate through team building.
- Increase the bond between the participants by working together in a close setting.

Overview:

The human knot is a team-building exercise used in leadership development courses to strengthen the bond between co-workers. In this setting, the human knot is used in lieu of a task that must be completed in the workplace.

This activity has certain risks associated with it that need to be identified prior to beginning. Using a pre-activity analysis is a powerful tool that encourages awareness and identification of hazards prior to beginning.

Pre-Activity Analysis:

1. Explain the activity directions and then give the participants five minutes to identify all the potential hazards and risks of solving the human knot. Potential hazards include:

    - back strain from bending down or reaching out
    - neck strain
    - hands or feet being stepped on
    - an elbow to the face
    - ergonomic-related injuries if the body is placed in an awkward position
    - slips, trips, or falls if the area contains any physical hazards.

2. Give the participants time to strategize how to complete the task in a manner that ensures no incidents or injuries occur.

3. Explain that participants will be in close contact with each other. If anyone feels uncomfortable with that, tell them to sit out and watch instead.

4. Start the task once everyone feels ready.

Activity Directions:

1. Ask the participants to form a circle facing one another.

2. Have each person reach out and grab another participant's hand. Then, with his or her other hand grab a different participant's hand. Each person should end up holding hands with two different people.
    - Encourage the participants to reach across the circle to connect with someone who is not next to them.
    - This will require the group members to be very close to one another.

3. Start to untangle the knot without breaking hands.
    - Participants can step over or under each other's grasp—whatever is necessary to untangle the group—as long as they do not let go.

4. If the group has not unwound the knot in five minutes, allow them to strategically decide on one pair of hands to separate momentarily in order to move the process forward. Once this move is made, immediately rejoin the hands that were separated. You can allow the group to do this again if they reach another impasse.

Debrief Questions:

1. What could we have done differently to get out of the knot better?

2. What were the hazards we identified before beginning this activity? Are any of these hazards present in the work environment?

3. Did we do a good job of working as a team to complete this activity? Why or why not?

4. What did you learn from this activity that you can apply in your work area?

Title: Communicating Obstacles

Time: 30–45 minutes

Materials:

| obstacles | chair | desk | backpack | garbage can |

For each team you will need:

a blindfold

Purpose:

- Understand hazard awareness.
- Practice communication, specifically, communicating the presence of hazards in the work area.
- Build trust among crew members.

Overview:

The most important component of working successfully in teams is trust. Without trust, teams are ineffective and potentially at risk. This activity focuses on building trust, improving communication among participants, and being able to direct co-workers away from hazards in the workplace. Trust is vital when watching out for each other; it is implemented through effective communication should co-workers wander into harm's way.

This activity is very safe when set up correctly. Be sure the room is large enough, the obstacles are generously spaced, and that the participants have a clear understanding of the directions and do not try to rush through the course. The course can be set up to the facilitator's liking, but make sure that there are enough obstacles to make course navigation somewhat challenging.

Prep Instructions:

Place various obstacles (such as chairs, desks, or backpacks) throughout the room.
- There should be ample space between the obstacles in a room large enough to accommodate the course.

Activity Directions:

1. Divide the group into pairs.
   - Group participants who do not know each other as well to help build trust.

2. Give each pair a blindfold.

3. Explain that the blindfolded participant must navigate successfully through the course with the help of his or her partner. The partner is responsible for providing clear directions, but may not touch the blindfolded participant. Remind the participants that it is critical for the partner to provide very specific directions so that the blindfolded person does not run into any of the obstacles. Encourage the blindfolded person to proceed slowly, maybe even walking with his or her hands out in front to ensure no interaction with obstacles.

4. Allow the first pair to begin navigating through the course.

5. After about 10 seconds, have the next pair proceed. Continue until all pairs have navigated through the course.

6. Repeat for the other partner.

Debrief Questions:

1. What was difficult about this activity?

2. How well do we communicate with one another in the field?

3. What do you need to do to make sure you are aware of dangerous obstacles in your work area?

4. What can you do to improve communication?

5. Do you trust your co-workers, and if not, what needs to be done to establish and ensure universal trust in the workplace?

Title: Relay Race: Maintaining Speed and Control

Time: 10–15 minutes

Materials:

three cups   masking tape
of water

Purpose:

- Create awareness that sometimes working too fast can slow you down in the long run (or cause problems in workflow downstream), because the task at hand is not performed properly.
- Weigh the ramifications of valuing speed more than accuracy.

Overview:

Haste makes waste. Slow and steady wins the race. While efficiency in the workplace is an important component of company productivity and meeting deadlines and budgets, working too quickly or sloppily can have a negative long-term impact on overall company performance and personal and co-worker safety.

Prep Instructions:

1. Fill three cups to the brim with water.

2. Tape a starting line and two sets of three to four "X"s on the floor, four to five steps from each other.

Team 1	Team 2
X	X
X	X
X	X

Activity Directions:

1. Divide the participants into two equal teams and have each assemble behind the starting line.

2. Give the first person on each team a full cup of water.

3. Explain the directions:

    - This is a relay race. The winning team is the one whose members complete the circuit first. While this is a race, the goal is to maintain complete control of the full cup of water and to use appropriate speed.

    - Each team member is responsible for navigating around the Xs on the floor. Each team member must complete a full circuit—from the starting line to the final X and back.

Team 1	Team 2
\ x /	\ x /
✕	✕
(x)	(x)
(x)	(x)

    - The full cup is then passed to the next team member who completes the circuit.

    - The process is repeated until each team member has completed the circuit.

    - If any water falls from the cup, the person must return to the starting line, refill the cup, and begin again.

4. Start the race and watch for any water spills.

    - The third cup of water is for refilling the cup after a participant spills. This way the cups are always filled to the brim during the race.

5. The first team to have each member complete the circuit is the winner.

6. Conduct a discussion about how working too fast can actually slow you down in the long run, because inappropriate speeds can lead to an accident, injury, or mistakes and inefficiencies on the job.

Debrief Questions:

1. Why do you rush through your work and how can you prevent rushing?

2. What can you do to ensure you are consistently operating at the appropriate speeds?

3. What are the hazards associated with operating at a rushed pace?

4. How can you encourage people to slow down when you see them rushing through their work?

5. Why is it better to do the job correctly and slowly the first time, versus rushing and having to do re-work?

Title: Safety Speed Dating

Time: 15–20 minutes

Purpose:
- Interact and communicate with fellow participants.
- Learn about safety procedures and each other.

Objective:

In this activity participants learn about each other and share ideas about safety topics. Participants may learn about safety procedures they did not know existed, or find ideas for safety that they may want to implement in their own work.

Activity Directions:

1. Divide the group in half and have the two groups form circles—an inside group and an outside group. The people in the inside should face the people in the outside group.

2. Have the outside group ask the inside group questions.
    - Possible safety questions:
        » What is a safety procedure that you frequently conduct?
        » What are three safety items that are most crucial for your job?
        » Describe an incident where a hazard was created because a safety procedure wasn't followed.

3. Have the inside circle rotate after one to two minutes so they are facing a new person. Repeat the process with the new outside person.

4. Continue this process until the inside group has completed the full circuit.

5. Have the groups switch roles—the inside group will now ask the questions and the outside group will answer and rotate until the circuit is complete.

Debrief Questions:

1. What did you learn about your peers through this activity?

2. Why is getting to know one another so important?

3. Do you trust your fellow employees? If not, what needs to happen to help build that trust?

4. How hard was it to share with your peers?

Title: Blindfolding Rectangles

Time: 15–20 minutes

Materials:
For each group you will need:

four blindfolds   two long strips
of ribbon (string
or other similar
material can be
substituted if
necessary)

Purpose:
- Increase communication and listening skills.

Objective:

We often have limited time and space in our workdays to focus on safety. As a result, we must learn how to use words carefully to delegate tasks and give clear instructions with our safety concerns embedded. In this exercise participants learn to use their words carefully to create the desired outcome.

• •

Activity Directions:

1. Divide the participants into groups of no more than five.

2. Explain that the participants are going to make two overlapping rectangles on the ground using ribbon. They will also be blindfolded.

3. Show the participants a picture of the overlapping rectangles, like the one to the right:

4. Select one person from each team to be the instructor. This person will not be blindfolded, but can only say 120 words to assist the blindfolded participants. As soon as the remaining participants have been blindfolded, every word spoken by the instructor must be counted. Once the 120-word limit is reached, the activity will end.

· ·

Debrief Questions:

1. How did you do at completing this activity?

2. How does this activity connect with safety?

3. Did you have a strategy in place before beginning the activity? If you had a strategy would that have helped?

4. What were the biggest obstacles that affected performance? Do these obstacles exist in the field? If so, how do you overcome them?

Title: Recipe Activity

Time: 15 minutes

Materials:
For each participant you will need:

paper   markers

Purpose:
- Identify the characteristics of a high-performing team.

Objective:

It takes many elements to keep a team functioning properly and safely. In this exercise participants think about what ingredients make up a high-performing team.

• •

Activity Directions:

1. Give a piece of paper and a marker to each participant.

2. Explain that the participants are going to create a "recipe" for the ideal team.
    - This activity should be completed individually because this will create more diverse recipes for a high-performance team.

3. Ask each participant to write a recipe for a high-performance and safety-focused team just as a recipe for a food item is written. Make sure everyone notes the ingredients and how to incorporate the ingredients together.
    - Possible ingredients include communication, respect, accountability, hard work, awareness, and inspections.

4. Give the participants 10 to 15 minutes to write their recipes.

5. Ask the participants to share their recipes with the group and discuss how they would combine the ingredients to create an effective, high-performing team.

. . . .

Debrief Questions:

1. What did you learn from your recipes?

2. How can you implement these recipes in the field?

3. What similarities were there with the recipes?

4. What were some of the most important ingredients?

5. Is there a way to hang these recipes in the workplace as a reminder of what to do?

Title: Operation Game

Time: 20–40 minutes

Materials:

For each team you will need:

| Operation board game | Lockout Tags | Copy of Lockout Procedure |

Purpose:

- Demonstrate the importance of making sure dangerous environments are safe from the beginning.

Overview:

The purpose of this activity is to promote proper lockout. There are potential electrical hazards present in many of our work areas and ensuring electrical safety can be the difference between someone going home safely and someone going home severely injured. This activity helps people understand the importance of electrical lockout, while demonstrating what happens when we rush into tasks.

Pre-Activity Analysis:

1. Split the group into small teams of three to six people.

2. Have each team review the company's lockout procedure.

3. Ask each team to answer the following questions:

4. What are the steps required to complete a proper lockout?

5. Why is lockout so important?

6. What are some tasks that might require a lockout?

7. Start the electrical training activity once everyone fully understands the lockout procedure.

- -

Activity Directions:

1. Pass out the board game Operation to each team.

    - Highlight that this is a competition and will showcase their electrical safety skills.

2. Explain the rules of the game:

    - The team that removes all the pieces first wins.
    - Flipping the board upside down is not allowed.
    - Each team member will take turns removing a piece using the tongs.
    - Anyone who is "buzzed" while removing a piece is dead and can no longer participate.

3. Tell the teams to start as soon as you give the directions.

4. Count the buzzes while the teams are working.

5. After the game is over, ask each team to share how many members died.

6. Ask whether any teams decided to lockout the game before starting.

    - Operation has an off switch the teams could have used before starting the activity.
    - Most teams will not have used this feature, despite discussing the importance of locking out minutes before.
    - Discuss that all teams should have turned off the game before beginning, rather than working on it live.

7. Congratulate any teams that did use a lockout procedure.

- -

Debrief Questions:

1. Did your team follow proper lockout procedure?

2. Why is lockout important?

3. What are the consequences of rushing into electrical work without taking the proper precautions?

4. Does anyone have a related experience he or she would like to share?

Chapter 4
Creativity Focused

These activities will be the hardest for your trainees to embrace, but they will have the most powerful impact. Most people believe they are terrible artists—and we usually don't like to do things we are not already good at—so when they are asked to draw things they grumble. Unfortunately this reluctance to participate prevents them from tapping into their creative side.

Creating art, however, is an amazing experience that provides a visual representation of the subject matter, which helps tremendously with retention. The goal for these activities is not to create mesmerizing art, but to create something visual that will help build the connection between the participant and the topic.

One very important thing to remember while conducting any activity that requires the participants to stretch their creative muscles is that people often feel self-conscious when doing something unfamiliar. Thus, the activities in this chapter may generate some initial resistance among your participants. It is important for you to explain the importance of trying new things and thinking and doing things out of the norm. While many of these activities work best with participants who possess a large amount of creativity, that is not a requirement. You should make it very clear that no one will be judged on artistic ability, in order to create a safe environment.

Title: Safety Superheroes

Time: 10–15 minutes

Materials:

For each participant you will need:

paper   colored markers

Purpose:

- Provide the opportunity for the participants to exercise their artistic skills (and use the other side of their brain).
- Encourage creative thinking.
- Identify ways to make the workplace safe from possible hazards.

Overview:

At some point during our lives, most of us have either envisioned or pretended to be a superhero. Our superheroes may have possessed super speed, super strength, or some other power dedicated to ensuring the wellbeing of others. This activity allows participants to envision their own superheroes, but with a safety spin.

By thinking about superheroes with safety-related powers, we can think about safety in a new way—it takes on superhuman effects. This will also help the visual learners connect more deeply with the task and remember the material more easily.

Participants may show a little hesitation, but after a few minutes, the majority of them will be very engaged in the assignment. When the learning environment is safe and encouraging, the participants will truly enjoy this activity. You can also post the superhero drawings around the room after the activity is completed and reference them throughout the training program.

• •

Activity Directions:

1. Give each participant a piece of paper and ask him or her to write down the name of a superhero with special powers who makes the workplace safe.

   • For example, Pyrokinesis, a superhero with the power to control fire with his mind.

2. Have the participants draw a picture of their superhero.

   • The drawings should be as detailed as possible, clearly displaying the powers.

3. Ask the participants to hold up their finished drawings, and explain their superhero's powers and why they chose them.

   • Pyrokinesis:

      » This superhero could be a man or woman dressed in orange and red, maybe with a flame-type logo.

      » His power (controlling fire with his mind) allows him to put out a fire before it makes contact with a worker.

• •

Debrief Questions:

1. What were your favorite superheroes?

2. What hazards did the superheroes combat? What tools are available to combat these hazards in our workplace?

3. How can you be a real-life safety superhero?

Title: Safety Sketch

Time: 10–15 minutes

Materials:

For each participant you will need:

sticky notes   paper   colored markers

Purpose:

- Learn how to communicate through art.
- Encourage participants to describe their work and share one important insight about safety.

Overview:

This activity works best in groups where the participants know each other well. It also works well with groups who are open and are willing to try new things. This activity requires participants to draw—not so much to create a masterpiece, but to describe safety in a visual manner.

Prep Instructions:

Write some safety items on sticky notes. Possible items include:

- flashlight
- pre-operational inspection sheet
- fall protection
- caution tape
- signage
- labels
- training

- safety gloves
- awareness
- fit for duty
- sixth sense
- hearing protection
- experience
- teamwork.

- -

Activity Directions:

1. Give a sticky note with a safety item written on it to each participant.

2. Pass out the paper and markers and explain to the group that they will be responsible for drawing a picture of the safety item on their sticky notes.

3. Have the participants draw their safety items.
    - Give them five to 10 minutes to finish.

4. Collect the illustrations and hold them up one at a time to let the group observe the drawings.

5. Ask the group to guess who drew each picture.

6. Ask each participant to tell the group which drawing he or she drew. Have each participant explain how the image describes and symbolizes a corresponding safety procedure from the workplace.

- -

Debrief Questions:

1. Who had the best drawing?

2. Do you do a good job of using these tools in the workplace?

Title: Safety Flags

Time: 20–30 minutes

Materials:

safety
magazines
(if available)

safety images
(printed from
the Internet)

For each participant you will need:

flipchart paper   colored markers   glue or tape   scissors

Purpose:

- Create a representation of safety as envisioned through the eyes of the participants.
- Produce a safety poster that can be displayed in the work area as a reminder of how to perform the job the right way the first time.

Overview:

Art is a powerful way to demonstrate ideas, beliefs, values, and principles. Many people have strong visceral reactions when they see art, because it allows them to easily connect with the message. This activity allows participants to produce safety-related and safety-inspired art that can be displayed in the work area.

A country's flag commands a lot of respect—it is a symbolic representation of its people and all they embody. In this activity participants will create a symbolic safety flag.

Activity Directions:

1. Give each participant a large piece of paper and colored markers. Distribute the safety magazines or safety images, along with the scissors and glue or tape.

2. Have the participants draw flags featuring symbols and images that define and illustrate the safety items they use and safety procedures commonly conducted in their workplace.
   - They can also use the magazine pages and printed images to decorate their safety flags.

3. Give the participants 10 to 15 minutes to create their flags.

4. Ask the participants to share their flags with the rest of the group and describe the images and symbolism contained within them.
   - This will likely generate some meaningful discourse regarding safety themes, priorities, and personal stories.

5. Display the flags around the workplace.

Debrief Questions:

1. Why did you choose the items you did in your art?

2. Do you take pride in your work, why or why not?

3. How can you ensure that you are working toward the themes identified in your art?

4. What visuals should we have in the workplace to remind us to work safe?

Title: Pipe Cleaner Masterpieces

Time: 30–45 minutes

Materials:

For each participant you will need:

15 to 20 pipe
cleaners

Purpose:

- Build constant safety reminders.
- Have participants focus on one safety tool for an extended period of time.
- Create visuals for the workplace.

Overview:

Building visual reminders of safety items will enhance safety awareness in the workplace. Participants will take pride in the colorful safety cues they create and enjoy seeing them displayed in the workplace.

As much as this activity is focused on creating visual cues for the workplace, it is also about having participants take time to think about their safety item while they are creating it.

• •

Activity Directions:

1. Pass out 15 to 20 pipe cleaners to each participant. Have extra pipe cleaners available in case participants need more.

2. Give the participants 20 minutes to use the pipe cleaners to construct a safety item that they use on the job.

- Each participant must construct his or her own safety item, and be able to talk about it and why it is important.

3. Walk around the room encouraging participants to think about the safety tool they are building. Feel free to create an informal dialogue about safety while participants are creating their items.

4. Ask the participants to share why they chose the safety item and how it relates to their job and safety in the workplace.

5. Hang the participants' safety creations somewhere that is easily visible in the workplace area after the activity is finished.

. . . .

Debrief Questions:

1. How will you view your safety item or your co-worker's safety items differently after this activity?

2. Why did you create the item you did?

3. How could you effectively use the tools built in this activity?

Title: Personal Value Letter

Time: 15–20 minutes

Materials:

For each participant you will need:

two sheets   pens
of paper

Purpose:

- Reflect on why safety in the workplace is important.
- Discover why workplace safety is an important part of achieving personal goals and living up to personal values.

Overview:

When participants remember what matters to them and why, safety becomes personal. Remembering your personal values will provide motivation to stay safe.

• •

Activity Directions:

1. Pass out a sheet of paper and a pen to each participant.

2. Ask the participants to think about and write down their personal values.
    - Allow five to seven minutes for this.

3. Pass out another sheet of paper to each participant.

4. Ask the participants to write a letter to the people who mean the most to them. Have them base their letter on the following question: Why do you decide to work safely every day?

• •

Debrief Questions:

1. Is anyone willing to share his or her letter with the group?

2. What does this letter mean to you?

3. Who did you write the letter to and why?

4. How do you remind yourself why you need to work safe?

Chapter 5
Brainstormers

The theme of this chapter is idea generation and sharing. People typically do not lack answers or ideas, they just lack the necessary platform to share them. These activities provide the creative spark that is often required to discover many of the solutions for various safety topics.

These activities are usually most successful when done with large groups and a facilitator who is skilled at asking open-ended questions. You will also want to have a mechanism for capturing the generated ideas from the group. These ideas can then become talking points to generate further group discussion.

Title: 10 Things We Share

Time: 10–15 minutes

Materials:

For each team you will need:

paper   pens

Purpose:

- Allow participants to find common ground and identify shared experiences.
- Generate a diverse list of safety procedures in a short period of time that can then be discussed in more detail.

Overview:

When people are able to find common ground and identify shared experiences, they are often able to open up communication channels and bond over their similarities.

Depending on the job, there are hundreds of different safety procedures that must be followed. Some of the more universal safety procedures, such as wearing seatbelts, using three points of contact, and walking slowly around corners, should be easy to identify. This activity challenges the participants to identify technical or specific procedures that might be more difficult to recall.

· ·

Activity Directions:

1. Divide the participants into teams of three or four.

2. Give a piece of paper and a pen to each group.

3. Ask each team to think of as many different safety procedures as they can. However, they can only list procedures they have **all** practiced in the

workplace—if a member of the team has not followed the specific procedure, it cannot be included.

4. Give the teams five to 10 minutes to complete this task. Encourage them to think of more than 10 items.

5. Count the number of safety procedures each team comes up with. The team with the most will be the winner.

• •

Debrief Questions:

1. Which safety procedures did you share?

2. Which of these do you do a great job of utilizing and which do you need to pay more attention to?

3. Why is it critical to constantly use these procedures?

Title: Safety Circle

Time: 5–10 minutes

Purpose:
- Think of as many safety-related items as possible.
- Establish a competitive environment that leads to involvement and excitement from the participants.
- Utilize a brainstorming activity that does not require any materials.
- Think about the breadth of safety-related items—things like water bottles may be essential to safety on a hot day.

Overview:

This activity is competitive and very effective with medium to large groups. The goal of the activity is to challenge participants to think of as many things related to safety as they can within a specific period of time. The participants compete against one another to determine who can think of the most safety-related items.

You will need at least six participants and enough space for everyone to spread out and form a circle. Be sure to give the participants a minute to think of some safety-related items before you start.

Activity Directions:

1. Have the group form a circle.

2. Go around the room and have each participant share his or her name, place of work, and occupation.

3. Ask the participants to think of workplace items related to safety. These can range from tools to procedures to behaviors to regulatory standards and so on. A few examples include:
   - inspections
   - awareness
   - being prepared

- training
- working together
- PPE (personal protective equipment)
- gloves.

4. Give the group a minute to think of some safety items.

5. Outline the rules of the activity:
    - One participant will begin by naming a safety-related item. Next, the person on the left will immediately say a different safety-related item.
    - This process will continue around the circle.
    - No participant can repeat an item that was previously mentioned. If this occurs, the participant who repeated the item must leave the circle and sit down.
    - The process continues until there is only one participant standing—that person is declared the winner.

• •

Debrief Questions:

1. What were some of the safety items mentioned in this activity?

2. Which of these items do you need to use on a regular basis?

3. What are some important safety items we did not mention in this activity?

4. We identified a lot of safety items, how can you remember them all so you know when and how to use them in the appropriate situations?

Title: Fears in a Hat

Time: 10–20 minutes

Materials:

hard hat or
baseball cap

For each participant you will need:

note cards   pens

Purpose:

- Provide a safe environment in which participants can share their fears related to safety.
- Foster constructive dialogue among peers regarding fears associated with their work.

Overview:

It is difficult for people to talk about their fears; it exposes vulnerability and can be very personal. However, it can also be cathartic and empowering for participants to share the concerns they have about their work. Having this confidential forum creates a safe environment for participants to share vital information with one another.

The objective of this activity is not to determine who said what, but rather to allow for important topics related to work and job responsibilities to be discussed within the group. Each fear identified by the participants should be discussed. When a fear is identified by more than one person, the facilitator should inform the group and ask if anyone would like to discuss it further.

Activity Directions:

1. Pass out a note card to each participant.

2. Ask the participants to write down any anxiety or fear they experience while performing their job function in the workplace.
   - Examples:
     - » falling from a great height
     - » sustaining a deep cut or penetrating wound
     - » being exposed to harmful gases.

3. Give the group a few minutes to document their fears and then ask them put their note cards into the hat.

4. Select a participant to choose a card and read it to the group.

5. Ask the following question: What things can we do to prevent this fear from ever becoming a reality in the workplace?

6. Have the group share their ideas on what can be done to prevent the safety risk from occurring. Continue the process until all the cards have been read.

Debrief Questions:

1. How do you overcome these fears?

2. Why did you identify these as the fears?

3. What should you do if you are feeling fearful at work?

Title: Safety Clips

Time: 10–20 minutes

Materials:

box of paperclips

Purpose:

- Have participants brainstorm the reasons for working safely.

Overview:

This activity is simple—ask each participant to take as many paperclips as he or she thinks will be necessary for the activity. This is the **only** direction the facilitator will provide to the group, other than requiring a minimum of three to four paperclips. The participants will probe for more direction, but it is important to keep the direction abstract and leave it entirely up to them to decide how many paperclips to take.

The participants must then share the reasons why they work safely—providing one reason for each paperclip they took. The facilitator may use the questions listed below to prompt participants who struggle to think of reasons for working safely.

• •

Activity Directions:

1. Ask the participant to take paperclips from the box: "As many as you think you will need, but at least three or four."

2. Explain to the group that they will be sharing one reason per paperclip for why they choose to work safely.
    - Paperclip 1: My wife, Jen.
    - Paperclip 2: My son, Jason.

- Paperclip 3: My granddaughter, Kelly.
- Paperclip 4: So I can drive my Corvette.
- Paperclip 5: So I can continue to travel the country.
- Paperclip 6: So I can continue to BBQ with my family.
- Paperclip 7: So I can continue to watch my favorite movie.
- Paperclip 8: So I can spend my money on the things that make me happy.

3. Have each person share why he or she works safely.

4. Use the debrief questions to help participants who are having trouble coming up with reasons.

• •

Debrief Questions:

1. What is a favorite food you would miss eating?

2. Have you visited all the places that are on your bucket list?

3. What things do you enjoy doing now that you would miss if you were severely injured?

4. Is there a favorite movie you would not be able to watch anymore?

5. Are there any dreams you plan to make a reality?

6. What are the names of your family members or friends?

7. Do you have a favorite car that you have not been able to drive yet?

8. Are there any hobbies you would miss?

9. What is a goal you have not yet achieved?

Title: Round Robin Word Association

Time: 10–20 minutes

Materials:

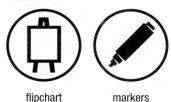

flipchart   markers

Purpose:

- Create mental connections using word association.
- Provide a safe, competitive, and collaborative environment.
- Generate ideas for future discussion.

Overview:

A round robin exercise involves all the participants and fosters healthy competition. The key to this activity is thinking of safety-related words that have a numerous associations. Participants who have the ability to think outside the box will have the most success with this activity.

Activity Directions:

1. Explain that the group will battle wits in a word association activity focused on safety until there is only one person left.

2. Have the participants stand and form a circle.

3. Select a participant to begin the word association activity.

4. Say a word or phrase out loud.

5. Ask the participant to say a word that is related to your word or phrase. Then ask the person on the right to share a new word associated with your word or phrase.

- For example, you start with "bad weather conditions":
    » participant 1: lighting
    » participant 2: temperature
    » participant 3: clothing
    » participant 4: awareness
    » participant 5: windshield wipers.

6. Write down each word the participants say on a whiteboard or flipchart.

7. If a participant makes one of the following errors he or she will be eliminated:
    - repeating a word that has already been said
    - taking longer than five seconds to say a word
    - saying a word that is not clearly related to the original word or phrase.

8. Each time a participant leaves the circle—either due to repeating a word, saying a word that has no connection, or not being able to come up with a word within five seconds—the facilitator will introduce the next word to the remaining participants, starting with the person to the right of the participant who last left the circle.

9. After the winner is identified, spend some time talking about the connections associated with the word or phrase.

• •

Debrief Questions:

1. Did this exercise teach anything you could use to improve your safety?

2. What other ideas and connections did this activity foster?

3. What phrase do you think had the most impact?

Title: Internal Tools Brainstorm

Time: 8–15 minutes

Materials:

flipchart

For each team you will need:

paper   pens

Purpose:
- Create an awareness of the internal safety tools we all possess.

Overview:

Too often we think of safety tools as physical objects. However, some of the most important safety mechanisms are internal. They helped us survive throughout human history. Those same skills and abilities that nature has endowed us with can and should be used to keep us safe at work. This brainstorming session will remind people of the tools they carry with them wherever they go.

. . . .

Activity Directions:

1. Divide the participants into groups of four to six.

2. Ask each group to come up with answers to the following question: What are some internal tools that help us prevent accidents?

3. Give the groups five to seven minutes to brainstorm.

4. Ask each group to share its list.
   - Possible answers include:
     - » hearing
     - » smell
     - » touch
     - » sight
     - » balance
     - » communication.
     - » intuition
     - » experience
     - » confidence
     - » brain
     - » common sense

5. Spend some time discussing why each tool is important.

6. Ask the group to discuss how they can use these internal tools to prevent accidents.

• •

Debrief Questions:

1. Which of these internal tools do you use well?

2. Which tools do you use all the time?

3. Which internal tools do you need to use better?

4. Which of the tools identified is the hardest to use? Why?

Title: External Tools Brainstorm

Time: 8–15 minutes

Materials:
For each team you will need:

flipchart   paper   pens

Purpose:
- Develop an awareness of the tools that make work more efficient and safe.

Overview:

There are many tools that can contribute to a safe environment when properly employed. This activity helps participants think about everything they use to keep them accident free.

. . . .

Activity Directions:

1. Divide the participants into groups of four to six people.

2. Ask each group to come up with answers to the following question:
    What tools do we use to prevent accidents from occurring?

3. Give the groups five to seven minutes to brainstorm.

4. Ask each group to share its list.
    - Possible answers include:
        - » ergonomic chairs
        - » step stools
        - » fall protection
        - » training
        - » radios
        - » personal protective equipment
        - » respirators

- » hearing protection
- » proper clothing
- » fire extinguishers
- » supervisors
- » peers
- » wheel chalks
- » inspections
- » signage
- » labels
- » radios.

5. Spend some time discussing why each tool is important.

6. Ask the group to discuss how they can use these external tools to prevent accidents.

. . . .

Debrief Questions:

1. Which of these external tools do you use well?

2. Which tools are you using all the time?

3. Which external tools do you need to use better?

4. Which of the tools identified is the hardest to use?

Chapter 6
Comprehensive Activities

The following activities should be facilitated during lengthy training programs that require extensive material coverage. Each activity in this chapter lasts anywhere from 20 minutes to more than an hour, depending on the size of the group and the application.

These activities allow for substantial learning and—from our experience—inspire important aha moments.

Title: Stranded on a Deserted Island

Time: 20–25 minutes

Materials:

For each participant you will need:

paper   pens

Purpose:

- Incorporate survival tactics into a safety mindset.
- Use a memorable activity to encourage brainstorming and connection to safety.
- Encourage teamwork in small groups.
- Generate purposeful conversations about safety among participants.

Overview:

What would you want if you were stranded on a deserted island for an extended period of time?

This is a question many of us have pondered. It is interesting to explore what you believe to be the most critical items for both survival and personal gratification. This activity gets participants to consider this question in a slightly different way—they will plan their survival on and escape from the island using the safety tools they select.

This activity demonstrates that safety tools are important both within and outside the workplace. The tools used in the workplace are often the same tools that are used at home.

• •

Activity Directions:

1. Pass out pens and paper to each participant.

2. Ask the participants to imagine that they will be going to work, but can only bring two different safety items. Have them write down those items.

   - Possible suggestions:
     - » flashlight
     - » fire extinguisher
     - » utility knife
     - » potable water
     - » first aid kit
     - » standard operating procedures.

3. Divide the group into teams of three to four people.

4. Explain that each team is stranded on a deserted island and is only able to use the safety tools each member has included in order to survive and escape from the island.

5. Ask the teams to describe how they would use the safety tools to survive. Note that the island has ample water and fruit to sustain life for two weeks.

   - Encourage creativity! Reference the TV show *Survivor* to aid in their creative and collaborative planning. The teams should be able to identify ways to use the safety tools for survival purposes.

6. Ask the teams to share their survival strategies with the group.

7. Extend the activity to make the following association:

   - These tools are needed in order to survive in the workplace: They are critical to maintaining success by working safely. When used properly, these tools and others can help save lives and allow for productive, injury-free work.

• •

Debrief Questions:

1. In reality how do you best use your survival tools?

2. What is our current safety strategy? If there isn't one, what should the strategy consist of?

3. What techniques did you use to solve this problem? Do you use these techniques to solve problems in the workplace? Why or why not?

4. What innovative solutions can we come up with to help us improve safety in our workplace?

Title: Safety Speeches

Time: 10–30 minutes

Materials:

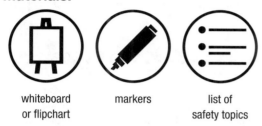

whiteboard   markers   list of
or flipchart   safety topics

For each participant you will need:

paper   pens or pencils

Purpose:

- Practice public speaking by presenting important ideas to the group.
- Provide participants with a more formal forum for sharing some key safety topics and messages.
- Challenge participants to move out of their comfort zone.

Overview:

This activity challenges participants to move beyond their comfort zone. The key to this activity's success is creating a safe and encouraging environment. Asking the participants to step out and expose themselves through public speaking will allow them to connect as a group on a much deeper level. People bond over shared challenges and this activity definitely qualifies as a challenging experience.

There may be a great deal of resistance—public speaking is one of people's greatest fears. Set the stage honestly by explaining that this activity is intended to push participants beyond their comfort zone in order to accomplish a challenging task. Create an environment where participants encourage their peers. Respect for one another is paramount to the success and intended objective of deeper camaraderie in this activity.

The intent is to have each participant speak for 60 seconds. It is essential for the facilitator to hold each participant to the 60-second timeframe. If anyone struggles to reach 60 seconds of speaking time, encourage the group to ask questions to help keep the speech going.

• •

Activity Directions:

1. Explain that each participant will be asked to conduct an impromptu speech. There will only be a small amount of time to prepare this speech, which can be funny or serious, depending on what the participant decides. The only rule is the speech much be related to the participant's topic.

2. Either assign the topic or provide each participant with two to three options.
   - Possible safety topics:
     - » flashlight
     - » pre-operational inspection sheet
     - » fall protection
     - » caution tape
     - » signage
     - » labels
     - » training
     - » safety gloves
     - » eye protection
     - » awareness.
     - » fit for duty
     - » sixth sense
     - » hearing protection
     - » experience
     - » teamwork
     - » proper lighting
     - » awareness
     - » reflective clothing
     - » right tools for job
     - » procedure manual

3. Allow no more than three minutes to prepare the mini presentation once the participants have their topics.

4. Select the first participant to present.
   - Have the speaker come to the front of the room to give the speech.
   - Start the timer when the speaker begins speaking.
   - Once 60 seconds is up, give the speaker a round of applause.

5. Ask the speaker to choose the next presenter—a reward for completing the task.

. . . .

Debrief Questions:

1. How did you do with this activity?

2. Where could you improve in regard to communicating in front of a group?

3. What were some of the takeaways from the speeches?

4. How many of you became more comfortable as the speeches continued?

Title: Newspaper Race

Time: 20–30 minutes

Materials:

For each team you will need:

a copy of the   scissors   highlighters
same newspaper
or publication

Purpose:

- Seek out and identify safety items, concepts, and practices.
- Understand that safety does not stop when you leave work, but is everywhere—in our homes, communities, cities, and so forth.
- Create competition among small groups.

Overview:

The safety of our friends, families, colleagues, and neighbors is vital to our continued growth and success. Safety is everywhere and can be spotted easily when looking through the right lens. The goal of this activity is to have the participants see safety as something ongoing that permeates our world both at and away from work.

Using the right publication for this activity will contribute to its overall success. A Sunday paper or other newspaper with many diverse stories and pictures is best. Another option is to use a magazine that highlights safety, or an industry-specific publication with multiple sections. You want participants to be thorough when going through the publication, so the more information and options they have, the better.

• •

Activity Directions:

1. Divide the group into teams of no more than four participants.

2. Pass out one newspaper or publication to each group. You must use the same newspaper or publication for each group.

3. Explain that the groups are responsible for finding as many safety-related articles and pictures within the publication as possible. They should cut out anything they find that is related to safety. If it has text, have them use the highlighter to identify the primary message related to safety.

4. Give the participants 15 to 20 minutes to identify their items.

5. Have each group count the number of items they found and debrief on the topics identified.

   - It is important to have each team explain how the items they selected are related to safety.

6. Declare the team with the most safety-related items the winner!

Debrief Questions:

1. Which stories stuck out most? Why?

2. What safety hazards exist both inside and outside our work environment?

3. How can we prevent some of the hazards identified in our work environment?

4. Were you shocked by how many examples of safety problems there were in the newspaper? Why or why not?

Title: Sharing Safety Moments

Time: 25–40 minutes

Purpose:
- Learn about other participant's experiences with safety.
- Impart knowledge through the art of storytelling.
- Establish connections between participants through sharing personal information.

Overview:

We all have safety stories related to either our own experiences or those of our co-workers. Stories have a powerful effect on us because we have our own unique connection to them. One of the best ways to learn is by sharing them.

The goal of this activity is to draw from participants' memories and have them share their safety stories with the group. These stories can be work-related, sports-related, family-related, and so on—the more powerful the story, the more impact it will have on the group. Encourage participants to think of experiences that have affected their safety in some manner.

Instead of simply opening up the stage to the group, the facilitator should share a powerful personal safety story first. Participants will be more likely to follow the facilitator's lead.

· ·

Activity Directions:

1. Set up the room in a way that ensures participants are comfortable and able to see each person in the group (a circle or U shape is best). The more inviting the physical space, the more effective the activity will be.

2. Give the group five to 10 minutes to think of a story or experience related to safety that occurred in the workplace.
   - This can be a story where a safety item saved someone's life or when a safety procedure was not followed and there were serious consequences.
   - Encourage the participants to think of a **powerful** experience—one that has had a lasting influence on them.

3. Share your safety story.

4. Ask each participant to share his or her safety story.

· ·

Debrief Questions:

1. What are some of the common safety themes?

2. How have these experiences changed your way of approaching work and life?

3. Share one thing you have learned today that you will apply to your work process going forward.

Title: Safety Bingo

Time: 25–45 minutes

Materials:

master list of   prizes
safety items

For each team you will need:

bingo cards   pens or markers

Purpose:
- Identify safety terms.
- Use the safety terms as topics for further discussion.
- Build value around the safety terms and items used in the game.

Overview:

This version of bingo is called SAFETY. It follows standard bingo rules.

This activity works best when there are prizes involved. Use it as a participant engagement tool, and then use the terms as a guide to talk about safety topics. To extend the activity, you can continue and play blackout bingo.

• •

Activity Directions:

1. Divide the group into teams and distribute a bingo card to each team.

2. Randomly call out items from the list of safety terms. Cross them off as they are mentioned and give the participants enough time to mark the term on their SAFETY card.

3. The first team to have six items across or five items down must yell "SAFETY" to win.

   - If any of the cards are the same, it is important to identify which team says "SAFETY" first!

4. Take some time to review the terms and safety implications surrounding them.

• •

Debrief Questions:

1. What did you learn from this activity?

2. When you return to work will you remember this activity? Will it make a difference?

• •

Terms:

- exit sign
- good housekeeping
- CPR
- good communication
- PPE required signage
- warning labels
- hard hat
- brother's keeper
- fit for duty

- proper lighting
- training
- labeling
- hearing protection
- tied shoelaces
- railing
- face shield
- HazCom
- falling object protection

- clearing snow from walkways
- goggles
- three points contact
- steel-toe boots
- inspecting fire extinguishers
- seatbelt check
- work gloves
- using gut feelings
- ergonomic keyboard
- drinking water
- reflective vest
- drive to conditions
- lock-out-tag-out
- car horn signals
- proper barricading
- first aid materials
- right tools for job
- awareness.

Card 1

S	A	F	E	T	Y
exit sign	good housekeeping	CPR	good communication	PPE required signage	warning labels
hard hat	brother's keeper	ergonomic keyboard	drinking water	reflective vest	drive to conditions
lock-out-tag-out	car horn signals	proper barricading	first aid materials	right tools for job	awareness
fit for duty	proper lighting	training	falling object protection	clearing snow from walkways	goggles
three points contact	steel-toe boots	inspecting fire extinguishers	seatbelt check	work gloves	using gut feelings
labeling	hearing protection	tied shoelaces	railing	face shield	HazCom

Card 2

S	A	F	E	T	Y
car horn signals	labeling	hearing protection	proper lighting	fit for duty	brother's keeper
tied shoelaces	hard hat	right tools for job	work gloves	proper barricading	inspecting fire extinguishers
good communication	warning labels	goggles	ergonomic keyboard	railing	falling object protection
seatbelt check	awareness	HazCom	using gut feelings	first aid materials	drinking water
PPE required signage	clearing snow from walkways	face shield	exit sign	drive to conditions	CPR
three points contact	reflective vest	training	good housekeeping	steel-toe boots	lock-out-tag-out

Card 3

S	A	F	E	T	Y
reflective vest	PPE required signage	ergonomic keyboard	clearing snow from walkways	first aid materials	tied shoelaces
HazCom	awareness	brother's keeper	falling object protection	good housekeeping	seatbelt check
training	exit sign	drinking water	lock-out-tag-out	CPR	proper lighting
labeling	drive to conditions	steel-toe boots	car horn signals	inspecting fire extinguishers	goggles
work gloves	railing	right tools for job	good communication	using gut feelings	three points contact
hearing protection	fit for duty	warning labels	proper barricading	face shield	hard hat

Title: Star Gazing Awareness Test

Time: 20–30 minutes

Materials:

metallic star
stickers or
colored tape

For each team you will need:

paper   pens

Purpose:
- Create an awareness of participants' work surroundings.
- Make the workplace safer.

Overview:

Workers often think they are paying attention to all the little details in their surroundings. Unfortunately, this isn't always true—people often fail to thoroughly inspect their work areas when looking for possible safety risks. In this activity we show the participants how it feels to thoroughly look over a space. In order to find all the stars, the participants will have to turn up their attention to detail.

Prep Instructions:

Prior to the participants' arrival place six to 10 metallic stars in hard-to-find places within the work area.

- These should be placed up high, down low, behind things, and so on.

- The goal is for the stars to be difficult to find, in order to force the participants to very thoroughly inspect the work area.

Activity Directions:

1. Explain to the group that they will be participating in an activity focused on helping people learn to be aware of their surroundings.

2. Divide the group into three to four teams and give each team a piece of paper and a pen.

3. Direct the teams to spend 15 minutes finding the stars you placed in their work area.
   - Tell the participants how many stars you hid.
   - Explain that the stars are located in out-of-the-way places, so the teams must be thorough in their search and inspection.
   - Have the teams record the location of each star on the sheet of paper.

4. After time is up determine if all the stars were located.

5. Discuss any difficulties the participants had in finding the stars, and ask them to talk about their level of awareness of their work area.

Debrief Questions:

1. How often do you conduct an inspection as thorough as you did with this activity?

2. How aware are you actually in your work area?

3. How can you boost awareness?

4. What prevents you from seeing the hazards that exist in front of you?

5. What has to happen to ensure you never walk past a hazard?

Title: Building the Tower

Time: 15–20 minutes

Materials:

For each team you will need:

paper cups   markers
(at least 50)

Purpose:

- Learn to communicate in a team setting.
- Allow individuals to contribute positively toward a group goal.

Overview:

By dividing the participants into groups for a timed exercise with a competitive bent, we allow team dynamics to develop and encourage participants to navigate the joys and trials of working with a team.

Challenge participants to voice their opinions, play the role their team needs them to play, and contribute to creating a finished product they are proud of. Ensuring workplace safety requires teamwork and communication, and this activity builds upon those skills.

• •

Activity Directions:

1. Divide the participants into teams of four to six people.

2. Give each team a large supply of paper cups (at least 50 per team).

3. Explain that this activity is focused on teamwork, sharing knowledge, positive thinking, and time management.

   - Tell the participants to imagine the cups represent the building blocks of working together safely.

4. Tell the teams that they will be competing against each other.
   - If space allows, have the teams work in different rooms.

5. Write a word that represents working safely in teams on each cup in the bottom row.
   - For example, honesty, clarity, specificity, and confidence.

6. Have each team spend 10 minutes building a tower using the cups.

7. Judge the towers based on height, aesthetic appeal, and sturdiness, and then declare a winner.

. . . .

Debrief Questions:

1. How well did you work as a team?

2. What things could you have done to improve teamwork?

3. How was knowledge shared?

4. How do you make sure that the building blocks of safety are incorporated in your team?

Title: Fit for Duty Role Play

Time: 15–20 minutes

Purpose:
- Think about different circumstances that can interfere with one's ability to work safely.
- Create awareness about all the different reasons one may not be able to work safely.

Overview:

Employees are usually aware of the well-known obstacles to being fit for duty—for example, they cannot fully perform their duties in a safe manner while drunk or under the influence of drugs. However, they don't realize that being excessively tired can also have the same potentially disastrous effects. This role-play exercise forces participants to think about the range of things that may make them unfit for duty.

. . . .

Activity Directions:

1. Select two people to participate in the activity.
   - Make sure to choose people who are confident enough to role play in front of the group.

2. Explain to the volunteers that they will be acting out different scenarios for the rest of the group.
   - Possible scenarios:
     » tired
     » sick
     » hungover
     » under the influence
     » angry
     » distracted
     » withdrawn
     » nervous.

3. Ask the group to identify each scenario as the volunteers act it out.

4. Explain to the group that the scenarios are common in the workplace and can have negative effects on job performance.

5. Discuss ways to overcome these scenarios if they are encountered in the workplace.

. . . .

Debrief Questions:

1. What happens when you operate in the workplace when you are not fit for duty?

2. What should you do if you are not feeling fit for duty?

3. Is there a policy associated with fit for duty and if so what does it say?

4. Is there any other scenario you would like to see acted out?

Title: Stack 12 Nails on One

Time: 15–20 minutes

Materials:

For each team you will need:

a small board   13 three-inch
nails or 16
penny nails

Purpose:

- Increase awareness of the importance of being equipped with know-how before attempting to complete a task.

Objective:

Depending on the situation it can be fun to tackle a problem on your own. Life is full of mysteries, but at work it's often better and safer to ask for help from someone who has encountered a similar problem before.

In this activity participants are asked to find the solution to a problem that seems quite difficult without the help of someone who has solved it previously. When knowledgeable resources are employed, the puzzle goes from terribly difficult to simple enough for anyone to solve.

However, don't allow Internet or smartphone use—at first.

Prep Instructions:

Hammer just the tip of one nail into each board.

. . . .

Activity Directions:

1. Divide the group into small teams, depending on the amount of nails and boards available.

2. Pass out a board and 12 additional nails to each team.

3. Explain to the teams that they must find a way to stack all 12 nails on top of the nail that is sticking out of the board, without letting any of the nails touch the board.

4. Tell the teams they can consult the Internet, books, or an SOP to complete the task.

   • Most groups will not attempt to find references for completing the task.

5. If the teams do not think to check references, explain that the same mindset is common in the workplace when workers are asked to complete tasks that are unfamiliar to them. This can damage equipment and cause serious injuries to the workers involved.

   • The solution can easily be found on the Internet.

• •

Debrief Questions:

1. Do we do a good job of using our resources to solve problems or do we continue to blindly solve problems when the answers are available?

2. What resources do you have available to solve problems?

3. What currently happens when a problem arises and you do not have the answer?

4. Did you do a good job working together to find the solution to this problem? How could you have improved your teamwork?

Title: Safety Sales

Time: 15–20 minutes

Materials:

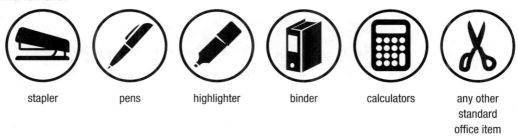

stapler   pens   highlighter   binder   calculators   any other
standard
office item

Purpose:
- Get group members to communicate and engage with each other in a creative way.

Objective:

Thinking about safety is rarely a fun or creative exercise—it's often about rules, regulations, and policies already in place. This activity requires people to think outside the box, and asks them to get creative about safety.

When participants let their imaginations run wild, they can come up with some pretty great ideas about how to stay safe. Even if the ideas are a little farfetched, or too difficult to implement at the moment, the activity draws attention to areas where safety could be improved.

This activity works well with participants who are skilled speakers. It will also help the more reserved participants practice speaking in front of others.

• •

Activity Directions:

1. Divide the group into smaller teams of three or four.
   - This activity works best with no more than four people per team.

2. Explain to the participants that this activity requires an imagination—the more creative they are, the more fun the activity will be.

3. Explain that each item "is no longer an office item but a futuristic safety item." Ask each team to think of a new fictional safety item with a futuristic fantastic ability.

   - For example:
     - » a role of tape = an instant cut healer
     - » a tennis shoe = a never slip shoe with super grip.

4. Have each team bring its item to the front of the room and try to sell it to the group. They must quote the price, the item's name, and its features and benefits.

• •

Debrief Questions:

1. What tools do you have available to overcome the hazards identified in this activity?

2. Which product was your favorite and why?

3. Do you use your safety tools enough? Why or why not?

Title: Hazard Pictures

Time: 15–20 minutes

Materials:

For each team you will need:

four to five pictures of dangerous work areas with many hazards showing. (These pictures can be easily found on the Internet.)

Purpose:

- Pay attention to detail.
- Identify possible hazards.

Objective:

Workplace safety may seem like a common sense issue, yet all too often we find that it isn't the case. In this exercise participants get to inspect other work settings to see what is going wrong safety-wise. It is not uncommon for participants to be shocked by what they see happening in other workplaces. This will make them grateful for what's done correctly at their place of work, and this activity will also help them keep their eyes open for future missteps.

• •

Activity Directions:

1. Divide the group into teams of three or four participants.
    - This activity works best with no more than four people per team.

2. Give each team the pictures and ask them to write down all the hazards or potential hazards they see in each picture.

3. Give the teams approximately five to 10 minutes to identify the hazards in the pictures.

4. Review which hazards the teams found and let them know if they missed any.

   - Many hazards and risks can be minimized or eliminated if workers are more aware of their surroundings and pay closer attention to the details of their work environment.

. . . .

Debrief Questions:

1. What hazards did your group find?

2. Do we have similar hazards in our workplace?

3. What can be done to prevent the hazards found in the pictures from creating injuries or incidents?

Title: Gauntlet Communication

Time: 40 minutes (includes set-up time)

Materials:

| foam noodles (at least three) | string or yarn | duct tape | a blindfold for each team |

Purpose:

- Practice clear and concise communication skills.
- Understand the value of detailed communication.

Objective:

In this activity giving good directions can make the difference between success and failure. This is often the case for delegating tasks safely. In order to assign a task and highlight the safety risks involved, good communication skills are needed. This activity requires people to speak directly and effectively and requires participants to listen actively in order to avoid unpleasant outcomes.

Prep Instructions:

1. Create an obstacle course using foam noodles.

2. Slide the string or yarn through each noodle and tape each end of the string to the ceiling, so the noodles swing back and forth like a pendulum.

3. Vary the height so that some noodles swing at head height, some at waist height, and some low to the ground, to make the obstacle course more challenging.

4. This activity can be structured however you like. The object is to have a blindfolded participant navigate through the course without being struck by the swinging noodles, using verbal direction provided by another participant or the entire group.

139

Activity Directions:

1. Divide the group into pairs and have them decide which person will be blindfolded and which person will provide direction.

2. Lead the teams, one by one, into the gauntlet area.
   - The blindfolded person should be blindfolded the whole time so he or she cannot see the location and height of the noodles.

3. Have the participant providing direction position his or her blindfolded partner in front of the first pendulum, and then step back and provide only verbal instruction through the obstacle course.
   - For example: The direction provider could say "duck to half height and take one step forward." The next direction could be to step over the next noodle, rather than ducking.

4. If at any time the blindfolded participant is struck by a noodle, he or she must start again at the beginning.

5. Repeat this process until each team has had a chance to navigate the obstacle course.

Debrief Questions:

1. What type of direction was the most effective?

2. What was the least effective?

Conclusion

Perhaps you've already put some of the activities in this book to work or maybe you are simply flipping through for the first time. Maybe your supervisor gave it to you knowing it could influence your role in your organization. You could be looking for some fresh ideas for your existing training program. Or, you could be looking to make a huge change to the status quo.

No matter how—or from where—you are approaching *Safety Training That Transfers*, we hope the book becomes an invaluable resource for you and has inspired you to see training in a new way. Any topic can be fun, engaging, and, most importantly, impactful to those who are participating.

We encourage you to engage your trainees, using active learning to make sure they leave the training programs with new knowledge and skills. Good training can have a powerfully positive influence and we have seen this time and time again with the clients we are blessed to work with. The activities in this book have worked for us and we very much encourage you to use them with your teams and colleagues.

Take the following success story for example. We once designed and implemented a training solution for one of our clients to enhance operator skills on a new, very expensive piece of mining equipment. We made sure that the equipment wasn't damaged and that all the new operators were extremely competent before signing off for them to begin operation. Our strategic approach helped the trainees ease the equipment into production both safely and ahead of schedule.

Writing this book is one of the most important things we have ever done. It strives to continue the already significant advancements that have been made in the area of employee development. We truly believe people have untapped potential that is best unlocked through training and support.

It has been our pleasure writing this book, and we thank you for taking interest in activity-based training. We wish you the very best in your journey and look forward to being a resource for anyone who wants to make sure their training gets transferred!

Good luck and have fun!

About the Authors

Steven Cohen is cofounder and CEO of Meyvn Global, a contemporary training consultancy with roots in the mining industry. He has logged thousands of hours focused on developing those in an organizational setting. Steve spends most of his free time thinking about the next great training solution, and is constantly building models for improving organizational health.

He is so passionate about creating a shift in the training paradigm that he has spent the past three years throwing every big idea that he has right in the face of convention. Working with clients throughout the world, Steve has positively influenced organizational performance with his creative mind and infectious energy.

Steve holds an MS in organizational development from Pepperdine University, and a BA in speech communication from the University of Illinois, Champaign-Urbana. He lives in Denver, Colorado, where he volunteers with Big Brothers Big Sisters, lives an active lifestyle, and takes every opportunity to fly to sunny California to visit with family.

Learn more at meyvnglobal.com or contact Steve at steven.cohen@meyvnglobal.com.

Ellis Ritz is a cofounder of Meyvn Global, and is currently acting as the director of learning and development. During his nearly 40 years of mining and training experience, Ellis saw a need for training and consulting on a level that others could better identify with.

Ellis is always looking for opportunities to get people more involved and to make training more enjoyable and memorable. He still does classroom training for trainers, frontline leaders, and safety classes, and is constantly working toward the day when all training gets a "hooray!" rather than an "oh no!" Ellis believes training can greatly affect the bottom line, save lives, and, through unique techniques, be fondly remembered and practiced.

Ellis holds a Certified Professional in Learning and Performance (CPLP) certificate through the American Society of Training & Development, now known as ATD, of which he is a member. He lives in Tucson, Arizona, where he writes short stories and poetry, and chases antiques when time permits. He retreats to fly-fishing when it's vacation time, as there is nothing like a new adventure.

Learn more at meyvnglobal.com or contact Ellis at ellis.ritz@meyvnglobal.com.